NEVER LEAVE
THE LOCKER ROOM
OF THE SUPER BOWL

Larry —
Congrats on your continued
success! . My my best!
Thanks —

BEN R. HANBACK

ISBN: 978-1-944878-43-6

Library of Congress Control Number: 2017944055

The sea throws rocks together,
but time leaves us polished stones…

-U2

While Ben hasn't played in a Super Bowl, he and his friends found their way in to the locker room in 1996 and lived in a moment few of us have. Ben understands the most basic need of people is to connect and feel connected.

Through a series of "connectable moments" he helps us ask some of the most important questions in our lives like:

What do I owe myself?
What do I owe those around me?
What do I owe the world?
What are the elements of a life well lived?

Give this book to your parents, your kids, your boss or your clients and connect with them in ways you might not have thought about before.

Colby Jubenville, Ph.D.

Ben sets the bar high, both in business and community service. He gives selflessly and accepts the responsibility of a leader that builds honest and positive relationships. This collection of articles is a combination of his experiences and the lessons he's learned. Through his lens, Ben encourages us to grow personally and professionally. I'm proud to be an FOB and honored to have had a front row seat as a partner and friend. Now, you have access to Coach Hanback!

Beth Torres, CEO
Make-A-Wish Middle Tennessee

Dedication

To Britt, love you.

Campbell and Bella – I love y'all more than you will ever know, thanks for making me a dad.

My parents, Chip and Barb Hanback, for your unconditional love.

My brother Casey, an amazing father and husband who taught me the love of the outdoors.

Adrienne and Bobby Oeding, for showing me the importance of spending quality time with family.

My grandparents, Read and Muriel Hanback, who taught me the importance of friendship and Earl and Dorothy Mortimore who taught me the satisfaction of a hard day's work.

Contents

FAMILY AND PHILANTHROPY

LEADERSHIP AND PERSONAL DEVELOPMENT

BUILDING YOUR TEAM

ACKNOWLEDGEMENTS

Introduction

I'm a storyteller. I love telling stories and I love remembering great times with friends, clients, and family. I've been blessed to have experienced some amazing events and been exposed to some incredible people.

I decided to share these life-changing experiences and began to regularly write about the lessons I've learned. This book is a compilation of that writing.

I've found that the only way to grow is to learn from the past and regularly take inventory of your experiences. My hope is that you can glean some insight from my stories and they help to make a difference in your life and in your business.

With that, I give you one of my favorite memories:

> "In 1996 my friends and I managed to work our way into the Dallas Cowboys locker room after their victory over the Pittsburgh Steelers in Super Bowl XXX.
>
> There we were. High-fiving Deion Sanders, watching Lesley Visser interview Troy Aikman, and at one point, holding the Vince Lombardi trophy. After about 45 minutes we decided to leave, thinking there might be another, better place to be. A party somewhere, maybe? But, after some time, we wound up standing behind Sun Devil Stadium thinking: 'What did we just do? Did we actually just walk out of the Super Bowl locker room? AGH!'"

Always enjoy the present moment, don't chase a better time, and never leave the locker room of the Super Bowl. Never.

TAKING YOUR CLIENT RELATIONSHIPS TO THE NEXT LEVEL

The Cheers Factor

I recently walked in to one of my favorite restaurants with a client and was greeted – by *name* – by the first three employees we encountered. My client leaned in and said, "WOW, you know EVERYONE here!"

Let's be honest … it is NOT that I know *everyone*. Instead, it's something I call the "*Cheers* Factor."

Remember when Norm would walk into Sam Malone's iconic bar *Cheers* and everyone would greet him by his first name? It was a welcoming gesture – and when applied in real life, makes a patron feel comfortable and validated.

Does your business have the "*Cheers* Factor"? If it doesn't yet, here are a few ideas to make sure your customers and clients keep coming back for more…

Under Promise, Over Deliver

This may be used all the time in sales, but has never been so applicable everywhere. One of the easiest ways to keep folks coming back is to surprise them and exceed expectations. My family went on a Norwegian Cruise Line vacation recently and we experienced exceptional customer service. During the trip, our concierge overheard us talking about how hungry we were in the afternoon and that we'd run out of coffee. Immediately, we had a tray of sandwiches and fruit in our room and extra coffee for the next day. After we returned home, I received a call from the cruise line thanking me for my business and offering me a personal contact and discount for my next cruise. This act ensured that when my family makes a decision to vacation, Norwegian Cruise Lines is at the top of the list.

Keep Your Client Engaged

"Out of sight out of mind" is a phrase that you should take to heart. In the fast-paced world of email and text it's easier than ever to stay in front of your clients. Try using a regular newsletter or an email blast to remind them of your products or services. My friend, Clint Smith, is the CEO of Emma and has structured his entire business around engaging the customer. Emma touts that they "organize your audience for maximum engagement." Make sure you're constantly in front of your audience so you don't fall into the "out of sight" trap.

Stay Transparent

Ever looked at an invoice, bill or receipt and think "why is this costing so much?" or "how much profit is really built into this?" In some industries like mine, fees, commissions and revenue are all disclosed, so the client knows exactly what their cost is. In other industries, this is not the case. I recently dealt with a contractor and got a quote for product and services that seemed very high and the price did not match the services, so I questioned it. They had a very hard time explaining the quote and in turn, lowered their cost. The more transparent you and your business are, the more comfortable your client will be.

Set Expectations

Setting expectations with customers is critical. My friend, Chris Morris, is an enrollment consultant and partner at Benefit Communications, Inc., and is one of the smartest business people I know. His business is enrolling companies in their benefit plans that are inherently complicated. He sets expectations on the front end, explains the process in detail and makes sure the client signs off on the timeline so there are no questions down the road. This makes for a smooth implementation process and repeat business.

Surprise Your Clients

If you haven't been to Sinema, the hot new Nashville restaurant and lounge, check them out. My wife and I recently went to dinner for our anniversary. The team at Sinema overheard us talking and the first round of drinks was on them *and* they seated us in a very private area, ensuring we would have a special evening. Are we going to go back? Of course we are – hospitality at its best.

Take these ideas to heart and it won't be long before your team is bursting with the "Cheers Factor."

Good Intelligence is Invaluable

My wife's uncle worked for the Secret Service for the majority of his career and I had one the most fascinating conversations with him a few years ago regarding his duties as an agent. He mentioned the power and importance of intelligence and information.

His example was simple: when he worked motorcade duty for a President or dignitary, there was constant radio contact. If there was a disturbance on a city street ahead they would notify the motorcade and divert the car to avoid the disturbance. Most times it was simply a group of kids or a rowdy group of protesters, but they would avoid the conflict whether it was potentially harmful or not. He explained that without good intelligence and information... you can be left helpless.

In life – and in business – information is critical. Good intelligence can be crucial to the success or failure of a business and career. Here are a few ways to make sure you are one step ahead of your competition.

Customer Feedback

The greatest source of intelligence you can gather about your team's performance is from your customers. Soliciting feedback on a regular basis and making changes or rewarding excellence is critical to your company. Bill Gates said, "Software innovation, like almost every other kind of innovation, requires the ability to collaborate and share ideas with other people, and to sit down and talk with customers and get their feedback and understand their needs."

Our organization sends quarterly surveys to our current clients asking for performance right down to the individual level. If you want to improve, make sure you have that great information straight from the most important revenue source your company has – your customers.

Employee Feedback

The second greatest source of information is right under your nose, and it's your employees! All great companies do internal employee surveys and react to feedback. Gates also said, "We all need people who will give us feedback. That's how we improve."

Here are some great reasons for gathering employee feedback:

- Making sure employees are engaged in the corporate mission. We have a saying in the insurance business called "presentee-ism" meaning employees who aren't engaged in their work are essentially absent. Keep your employees involved!

- Giving the employees a voice in what goes on in their company, department or team. You will often get ideas for improvement and cost savings from the folks that are on the front line. The TV Show *Undercover Boss* has proven this time after time.

- Growth. Plain and simple, you will not grow without the full engagement and commitment of your team.

Acting on the Information

Once you've gathered the intelligence, it's time to act. If the feedback received falls on deaf ears or your employees and clients don't see a change or improvement, your information was wasted.

I recently sat down with a vendor and they asked my feedback on everything from my experience as a customer, to suggestions to improve business, to ideas that I had for improving the overall customer experience. I saw immediate changes based on my feedback and comments. Remember, it's easy to take notes, but implementing change is what will make a difference.

Intelligence and information can be a powerful tool if received in a timely manner and used to stay on top of the competition and keep your employees happy.

Make sure you're staying a step ahead. Ask your customers how you're doing...or they may not be around to ask down the road!

Are You Selling a Product of Experience?

One of my family's favorite shows is *Shark Tank,* where entrepreneurs pitch their product or service to a panel of millionaires in hopes of snagging a business deal. I love hearing the critiques and feedback from Mark Cuban and the other Sharks – you'll often hear them say they love the idea or product, but the entrepreneur hasn't achieved enough sales to warrant an investment.

Now take a moment to think about yourself and your business. Are your sales where they need to be? Are you offering a product or are you offering an experience when a customer purchases from you? Consumers today are constantly bombarded with new products and services, so here are some ways that companies and business people are separating themselves from the pack.

Backstage Experience

If you haven't been to the new "blowout" bar – The Dry House – in Nashville, then you need to check them out. Owners Ali Ryan and Cassidy Bentley have created an environment where clients keep coming back for more. Guests can book an appointment online and select several hairstyles from zip codes across the country (i.e. The Nashville "615" is a "good ole southern blowout with attitude"). When you enter The Dry House, you're offered a drink and an iPad loaded with over 100 magazines. And it's certainly not your typical shampoo and hair dry, the atmosphere and special touches ensure that you leave with a true "Nashville backstage experience."

Touch, Feel, Taste

I often find myself wandering the aisles at Costco on any given weekend with my family (and yes, I secretly love it). As soon as you enter Costco, you forget you're in a warehouse because Costco has expertly created a unique consumer experience. Where else can you pick up a dozen roses, sample lobster bisque, try on a winter coat, play with the newest digital camera, and flip channels on an 80" flat screen TV? My friend, Dan Stephenson of Dan's Gourmet Mac & Cheese, just landed his product at Costco and is out on the road letting people taste and experience his amazing side dish before they buy. Costco knows how to truly engage and keep their client base.

Loyal Fans

My friend, Dierks Bentley, not only offers his fans a seat at his concerts, but also a true "experience" at his shows. His fan club (DB Congress) can meet him, hear a few intimate warm-up songs before the show, upgrade to VIP seating, *and* gain access to special one-of-a-kind autographed merchandise. He annually thanks his "Congress" at a fan club party where he signs autographs and takes photos for up to 5 hours – ensuring loyal fans and cementing repeat concert goers. Recently, even *The Grand Ole Opry* started offering "backstage tours" as a source of revenue and expansion of the fan experience – proving once again, that concert-goers, in particular, want more than just a seat at the show.

Autograph vs. Experience

Nashville and Middle Tennessee are two of the most philanthropic areas in the United States. In fact, if you wanted, you could attend a charity event almost every night of the week. I have been involved with the *Make-A-Wish Foundation of Middle Tennessee* since 2000 and a big part of our fundraising has included events showcasing auction items. Over the past few years, our patrons have shifted their interest from items like as gift baskets and autographs to "experiences." Tennessee Titans placekicker, the late Rob Bironas, would offer a personal kicking clinic at the Titans complex, as opposed to a simple autographed jersey or ball. This "experience" would raise big money and offered donors so much more than a simple take-home item.

The late Steve Jobs once said: "You've got to start with the customer experience and work back to the technology – not the other way around". Keep these words in mind when you think about your company and product. Regardless of what you're selling, start with the experience you want to create and work backwards. Make your clients feel like VIPs and watch your sales skyrocket.

Sharing the Customer Experience

You've seen it happen: a customer or client has a great experience and tells one, maybe two people...yet when they endure a bad experience they tell EVERYONE.

W. Edwards Deming once said: "Profit in business comes from repeat customers; customers that boast about your product and service, and that bring friends with them." With apps like Yelp! and online reviews of most products and services it's even more important to make sure you and your team are providing a great customer experience.

During the recent ice storm that Middle Tennessee experienced in February, one local employee made sure his customers wouldn't suffer. Butch Golson, the store director of the Harris Teeter in Westhaven, heard about the storms and immediately secured a hotel room within close proximity to his store. The move ensured that no matter how bad the weather got, Harris Teeter would stay open for business. Imagine how many times this story will be told and the loyalty that Butch has created for his community with his actions during a very challenging time.

Creating that great experience for your clients – one that makes them share far and wide with others – is harder than you think. And, a bad one can crush your business reputation quickly. So take notes because here are some people and companies who are making their customer experiences exceptional and memorable:

Modern Marine

Three years ago, my friend, Chris Williams and I bought a boat from Modern Marine. A few months later, owners Johnny and Jason Padgent asked us if we'd like to work at the boat show. Puzzled at first, we quickly realized this was genius marketing. Our name tags read "I am a happy Modern Marine customer and I would love to answer any questions!" Think about it, a consumer would much rather talk to a satisfied customer than a pushy sales person. We quickly found ourselves talking about how much fun our families had on the boat over the summer and the memories we were making vs. the features of the boat, gas prices and price tag. Needless to say we've worked the boat show ever since.

Country Music Hall of Fame and Museum

The Country Music Hall of Fame and Museum has experienced a tremendous rate of growth not only in space, but also in foot traffic. From 2013–2014, attendance increased from 668,777 to 970,991, and they expect to hit the million mark in 2015. The success wasn't only because of the popularity of Country Music. The museum takes extra steps to ensure visitors get a special experience and word travels quick. The addition of limited engagement exhibits that have included Taylor Swift, Carrie Underwood and Miranda Lambert, ensures relevance with younger music fans. Their *Words and Music* partnership with local schools allows area students to participate in songwriting sessions and try out various instruments. The expansion of the museum, retail space and move of the beloved Hatch Show Print to the building ensures each and every visitor a true "Nashville VIP" experience.

"Strategic" Hospitality

Benjamin and Max Goldberg of Strategic Hospitality go to extremes making sure their customers are happy. Their latest project, Pinewood Social, has quickly become one of Nashville's newest hot spots and it's not by accident. I had a dozen people mention their visit to Pinewood before I had the chance to pop in myself. You don't just eat or drink at Pinewood Social, you experience it…from the vintage bowling lanes, coffee bar, amazing menu, private karaoke bar, to a staff that pays attention to every detail, you'll definitely leave wanting more.

OZ Arts

Cano and Tim Ozgener and their family (former CAO Cigar founders) founded an amazing new non-profit: Oz Arts Nashville – a contemporary arts center located in the old CAO headquarters. They have made great strides in a very short time and it is due in part to the focus on their patrons. The Ozgeners have created a culture where the customer is treated like a true partner. For example, the audience is invited to a reception after every event to meet and mingle with the performers. Oz Arts spent countless hours looking at venues around the world and modeling themselves after the very best. Their organization and its formation was accomplished with the assistance from curators from MoMA and The Whitney in New York City. In turn, their work and dedication is creating a crazy buzz not only in the Nashville community but also the world.

Football Great Roger Staubach once said: "There are no traffic jams along the extra mile." Make sure you really go the distance for your customers and lock up life-long, happy clients that will spread *your* good word.

Show Me Your Clients and I'll Show You Your Future

This past year I was reunited with my childhood friend, Brad Benyak, of Dallas, Texas. After catching up on old times, we both agreed that if we lived in the same city today, our families would be fast friends.

While chatting, Brad shared Pastor John Kuebler's saying with me: "Show me your friends and I'll show you your future." Immediately I realized that in many ways, just like our friends define us, so do our customers. We all have an idea of what the perfect client or customer is – or should be. Here are a few simple ways to work with – and, in some cases, choose – clients who will ensure your bright future.

Communication

In any relationship communication is important, but when selecting a client it's critical. Have you ever been bidding for business or preparing for a presentation and the prospect isn't responding with the proper information you need, and won't return phone calls or emails? This is likely a sign of things to come. Make sure expectations are set ahead of time. In our industry, timely information is critical. A client can make you look bad very quickly, so make sure open communication is a VERY early foundation of your relationship.

Payments

Every business has fallen victim to a customer who won't pay bills, or is habitually late. The cause could be varied – poor management, cash flow issues, internal staffing issues, or laziness. We had a client a few years ago that fell three months behind with their insurance premiums and when we reached out, we didn't receive a response. We made the difficult decision to terminate the contract – and we made it quickly. When dealing with accounts receivable issues sometimes there's an easy explanation and your clients will thank YOU for bringing to light their own oversight. But it's always better to address the issues immediately and directly.

Price

Price is sometimes the lynchpin of a relationship – but it can also be the breaking point. If a customer chooses your organization for price alone then that's a sure sign they'll leave you for the same reason. Mark Blaze, President of Dex Imaging Tennessee, who is in a very competitive industry (copiers and imaging) donates a portion of their profits to local non-profit organizations that their partners support. This ensures not only long term value with Dex, but also an economic shot to the health of our community. Remember, part of choosing a great client is knowing they're partnering with you for the *value* your organization brings, in addition to a competitively priced product or service.

Partnership

The best client relationships are the true partnerships – they're a two-way street. Things are going to go wrong and mistakes are going to be made. I always tell our clients that problems are going to arise that may or may not be in our control, but we'll do our best to correct them immediately. A great client and true partner will understand this. At the same time, giving your customer the benefit of the doubt when things get off track will show them you're on board for the long run too.

Have Fun!

Yes, you can actually have fun and conduct business at the same. We tell our clients that we'll provide extreme customer service...

and we are fun to do business with! On a regular basis, we try and engage our clients in activities that are not only educational, but also fun and rewarding like charity events, seminars, even "customer field trips" to a sporting event or concert. Recently, we were invited to judge a client's pumpkin-carving contest on Halloween. We showed up in costume and had a fun morning. Make sure you spend quality time with some of the most important people in your life.

Your customers can and will define you and your business. Choose them wisely and I promise you and your organization can bet on a very bright future.

Thanking Clients

As most of my friends will tell you, U2 is my favorite rock band. My wife and I have seen them in concert numerous times over the years and even had the chance to take our children to a recent Chicago show. At the end of their concerts, just before the encore, Bono shouts to the crowd, "You've given us a great life...you've spent your hard earned money to be here...thank you." I can tell you that it's sincere and heartfelt.

How many times in your life have you wished you'd thanked someone and it slipped your mind? I'm guessing a lot! It's critical to remember how important this simple act can be to your friends, clients, or customers. Doing it in a genuine and professional way can be easily integrated into your business day:

Do Business with Them or Refer Business TO THEM!

One of the highest compliments you can give is to do business with the colleague you are thankful for or refer a client to them. When it makes sense, our firm tries hard to make our customers our vendors. Look at where you're spending money, realize you just might be able to save money and expand your relationship at the same time. A referral can be just as powerful. We try to send new leads to our current client base often – it's easy and can pay off big time.

Support a Cause Close to Their Mission

Find out what causes or charities your client supports. Are they hosting a 5K or gathering toys for a gift program? Either way, make sure you and your team are supporting them with your money or time. In fact, it doesn't have to be a charity event. In my first sales territory, I had a client with a son who played high school baseball and I would sit with him and watch the games. It was a fabulous way to spend time with my customer. Face-to-face interaction can't be replaced – and if you aren't there, your competition may be!

Call and Say "Thanks"

You've heard me talk about hand written notes because, frankly, I love 'em. It takes two minutes to pick up the phone and thank a client, leave a voicemail or simply check in and see how things are going. I've found that the more often you do this, the more an opportunity can arise for both of you to collaborate. And, if there's a problem lurking, you'll head it off at the pass.

Make Sure They Get Your Very Best

We've all seen this happen – our loudest clients get the most time from our teams, leaving our best clients with little to no attention. Make sure this doesn't happen. Treat each customer like they're your only one – or at least make them feel that way.

Surprise Them

This doesn't have to be flowers each birthday. In fact, sometimes the best gestures are totally unexpected. It could be delivering your order or product early, giving them a "friends and family" discount one month, calling them at the last minute for lunch or drinks. I had a vendor send me movie ticket vouchers because they'd heard me mention that my wife and I love to take our kids to the movies. As the old saying goes, "It's the thought that counts." Prove it.

So, just like U2 thanking their loyal fans at the end of a show, make sure you are grateful and authentic. Take the time to show appreciation for your relationships because you don't want them heading for the exit before YOUR encore!

MAXIMIZING RELATIONSHIPS

Being Nice in Business "Thanks Mom"

Spend some time with my mom, Barb, and I guarantee you'll hear her say "Be nice!" on a VERY regular basis. She's usually speaking directly to my dad, brother and I, who would engage in our fair share of parent/sibling quarrels.

As with most things, my mom was always right. Being nice to others is critical. And her reminders have always made their way into the way I handle business.

You may have heard the quote, "Nice guys always finish last." That phrase was based on a quote by baseball manager Leo Durocher and it was condensed by reporters in the 1940s. What he'd actually said was "The nice guys are all over there – in seventh place" (hint: seventh place meant last place).

Contrary to that popular phrase, I couldn't disagree more. I'd swear my mom was right and here are a few spots in business where being nice will surely put you in first place.

Share the Credit

Whether you're a CEO, part of a team, or in a sales role, at some point you'll be recognized for your efforts. It's human nature to jump out front and take credit for your achievements, but you probably didn't do it alone. Make sure you step back and give business partners that helped you along the way some love. It could be your customer service team, a group of manufacturers, or a strategic partner. In my industry, underwriters price most of our products and they often hold the key to your success or failure when pricing and marketing insurance products. I try and give them full credit when we have a big sale. Your partners will thank you for it and it will motivate them to work harder for you moving forward.

Louder is Not Better

In 23 years of business I've encountered plenty of vendors or customers who believe the louder you speak, the quicker things will get
done. I vividly remember dealing with a vendor who began shouting at
me on the phone about a business mistake he thought was a serious
issue, but in reality, was completely fixable. My immediate reaction
was to shut down. I promise you'll get further in any tough situation
by staying calm and friendly.

Smile Through the Phone

I honestly believe you can tell when someone is smiling on a phone
call. It comes through in their voice and attitude. Have you ever
walked up to a retail employee at a store and immediately tell if
they're have a good or bad day? I can always tell! A "bad day" can
be contagious. Try hard to avoid getting caught up in someone
else's problems. I've read it can take five nice compliments to make
up for one negative comment. Before you engage in a business
conversation with a client, think about being nice and treating
your client or customer like you'd want to be treated – let that
"good" day be contagious.

Embrace Conflict

Being nice doesn't mean avoiding a tough situation or being *soooo*
nice that you get trampled on. Regardless of how you treat people
or approach situations, you still have to make sure things get done.
I've caught myself at times holding back at a meeting where I felt
I might hurt someone's feelings. Remember, you can still be nice
and be honest at the same time.

It's Easy

Last, but not least, taking a gentler approach in business truly can
be a much easier path. I stay active in the Make-A-Wish Foundation – Dwayne "The Rock" Johnson, who has granted too many

wishes to count, said "Not only do I think being nice and kind is easy but being kind, in my opinion, is important."

It's made my path to success a "nice" one.

Mom was right.

Face-To-Face Meetings

I'm convinced that those of you with teenagers will relate to the story I'm about to tell you.

My wife and I woke up the other day and found ourselves living with an old, grouchy, retired couple …I mean…our teenage son and daughter. The once pitter-patter of little feet to greet me at the door after the end of long day is gone. Now, the couple living in our house walks around like silent zombies whom I yell at several times to come to the kitchen because dinner is ready. Even then, they grab their plates and head into their corners with the laptop or stare at the T.V.!

Recently, all four of us decided it was "dine-out" night and we ventured out to find a meal. We settled on our favorite Italian place close to home, and about half way through the meal I realized that we were actually having a meaningful family conversation. Talking about school, work, friends, summer vacation, plans for the week – it was refreshing. Even though we've evolved as a society, our families really need to try to stay consistent – making time for each other.

I've found that this also holds true in business. Even with the hectic pace of business decisions, there's still room and a need for face-to-face communication with clients and customers. Here are a few examples to help you get back to work…and across the table from the people most important to you and your business.

One-On-One

I recently had an appointment with a very large prospect and friend that is a company executive. Our meeting was rescheduled a couple times on both sides, when he suggested that we meet for lunch at his office. I was excited as I was going to get to see their new offices and typically I am the one hosting the lunch or dinner. It was probably one of the best one-hour business meetings I've ever had. Not only did we catch up personally, but also had the chance to discuss our careers, businesses and items of concern. This, in turn, led to business opportunities and projects where we could help each other…not only at our respective companies, but also in the community as well. It was an invaluable one-on-one. If you've haven't had a one-on-one with a client recently, then try it. You may be surprised and pleased at the outcome.

Path of Least Resistance

Thanks to emails and scans, it's become commonplace to fire over a proposal or communication to a client or prospect…and forget about it. Recently, I was about to send a quote via email. Instead, I picked up the phone and set up a meeting. The rest of the story…

When I met with my client, our conversation started with some serious concerns they'd had recently facing their business. These were concerns I know would not have surfaced if we'd emailed or even talked on the phone. Some concerns I was able to help with and others I was glad I was there to just listen. Entertainment executive Peter Guber said, *"Nothing replaces being in the same room, face-to-face, breathing the same air and reading and feeling each other's micro-expressions."* This couldn't have been truer that day. Make sure you're not overlooking an important client that may reveal more to you in person rather than through the intangible internet.

Trust, Attention…and Validation

Finally, remember that meeting in person gains attention, trust, and validation. Think about the last conference call or webcast you were on. What else were you doing? Checking email, talking to co-workers, working on another project? Have you ever been on a phone call and just knew the other person was pre-occupied or not engaged? A face-to-face meeting generally ensures everyone's full attention.

If you're a relationship builder like I am, then the ONLY way to nurture and build trust and validate a relationship is to meet in person. I was honored recently to hear Navy Fighter Pilot and P.O.W. Charlie Plumb speak about his experience in a Vietnam prison camp. He mentioned that alone and hungry in his cell, he did not feel validation as a human being until he first made contact with another American prisoner.

I recently introduced a group of clients and friends to each other as I felt they could mutually benefit from meeting. This couldn't be done by email or phone – they trusted me, and I validated that meeting – in person.

When all is said and done, email is easy. Face-to-Face is not. Strengthen relationships by putting yourself across the table from the people who are most important to you and your business. You never know what will happen!

Life is a Relationship Network

When my wife, Brittany, and I moved to Nashville in 1998, we immediately fell in love with the country music scene and became regulars on Lower Broadway and the Bluebird Café.

We went to a Halloween party that year with one of my colleagues, Sadler Norris and his friend. That friend was from Phoenix and had moved to Nashville to break into country music. Over the next three to four years, we followed that friend from bar to bar, supporting his music and his dream to make it in the relentless Nashville music business. Fast-forward to New Year's Eve just a few years later at Bridgestone Arena and Dierks Bentley was performing. Bentley yells to the crowd that this wasn't his first gig on New Year's Eve in Nashville ... that, in fact, he'd played across the street at dinner the previous year for Ben Hanback and his friends and then thanked us for our support!

Hands down, the greatest assets you have as a business professional are your relationships. Life is really a network, and you have to treat your friends, clients and vendors as if you'll have a relationship with them forever. You never know when you can help a friend, or when a relationship will benefit you down the road.

Here are some simple tips to solidify and ensure your relationships will be around for years to come.

Be There For the Good Times (and the Bad)

It's easy to celebrate when things are going great, but when times are tough, true colors often show through. When my friends and clients are in a career transition I actually write an unsolicited letter of recommendation. If they lose a job − or decide to make a career move − I prepare two copies of that letter. I let them know they can count on me as a business and personal reference, or simply for support. When times are tough, your friends or clients want to know you're there for them. Be there.

Thank You Notes and Birthdays

I'm going to sound like a broken record, but I still sit down at the end of the week and thank my new relationships and current clients with a nice note. Ask any of my friends or clients, and they'll tell you the last – and sometimes only – birthday card they received this year was from me. Now, think about it. The US Postal Service is about to stop service on Saturdays and the average American gets only one piece of handwritten mail every seven weeks. Make sure that piece is from you.

Build Bridges (Don't Burn Them)

Some people will say it's easy to dismiss a relationship and move on, however, I find it to be much the opposite. I make it a point to make sure I'm connecting with and introducing folks to one another – especially those I think may benefit each other down the road. I'm a member of the Entrepreneur's Organization (EO) and we have a regular discussion called "Needs and Leads." This is a way to tap into each other's business relationship and experiences – and fill a void that may exist in your business. Think about all your relationships and how you can help someone else fill a relationship gap that could benefit his or her business.

The Circle of Trust

I love the scene in *Meet the Parents* where Robert DeNiro explains the circle of trust to Ben Stiller. As I've grown in my business career, my circle of trust has been invaluable. I received advice early on to always maintain a close group of colleagues – I affectionately refer to them as FOB's (Friends of Ben). These will be folks you can count on throughout your career. Your own FOB's will be the people you count on for reinforcement and support as you grow. Choose wisely and keep them close. It'll pay off when you least expect it.

My friend, Dierks Bentley, has a song out called *I Hold On* – about keeping your family, country, and friends close, no matter how life changes. You should keep this message in mind because it's not just a great country song, it's a way to live your life, run your business, and treat your clients.

Dierks Bentley and Ben Hanback at the Drunk On Plane
video shoot in Los Angeles

Situational Awareness

Situational Awareness (S.A.) is a military term that is defined as the ability to identify, process, and comprehend critical elements of information about what is happening to a team in regard to a mission. Simply, it's knowing what's going on around you. For a soldier, S.A. – or lack thereof – could mean life or death.

I've observed that in our tech-consumed world, it's easy to lose contact with our surroundings. I call my own S.A. my "space radar." Like an alarm, it goes off when something doesn't feel right. I will walk in to a room or meeting and take survey of who's there and what's going on.

My family was on a weeklong vacation this past month in the Boston/New England area and I've never experienced more of a lack of situational awareness in my life. From the airport, to hotels and the bustle of a large city, people were so focused on their devices and completely unaware of what was going on around them…it about drove me crazy!

As in life, S.A. is absolutely critical in business. Here are a few ways to keep your "space radar" up and your frustration down:

Don't Assume

There's an old saying, "Don't assume anything as it will make an ASS out of U and ME." Our preconceived notions and assumptions can lead us down the wrong path…AND, more importantly… distort our awareness. I had a lunch appointment recently and we had never met in person. We were on a "blind business date" so to speak. When I arrived, I was seated first, and was anxiously watching people enter. A man in jeans and work shirt arrived and was seated by himself, but I was sure that wasn't my appointment as this was a senior executive I was meeting with. After almost 10 minutes, the man in the jeans came up to me asked "Are you Ben?" Turns out his team was volunteering at a local charity and he was dressed for the afternoon...and I overlooked him. My assumption was that he'd be dressed in a suit for our meeting. Don't let your past experiences or expectations distort your situation.

Frustration as Distraction

Frustration or anger can distort your situational awareness easily. Case in point, I was driving back to the office while on my phone having a very heated business discussion and a large white utility truck pulled up next to me honking their horn while the man inside yelled at me. I was in the heat of the moment and figured I'd cut him off or that I was swerving and had angered him... so I ignored him. We eventually came to a stop light and he was still honking and yelling at me, so I reluctantly rolled my window down and he said "Sir, you have a flat tire!!" Wow...talk about humility. I thanked him and pulled over. Remember, don't let frustration and anger distract you from your surroundings and the task at hand.

Observe and Communicate

Finally, two great keys to S.A. – make sure you observe your surroundings and communicate. I'm a big believer in observing and watching people's facial expressions...sometimes communication can come in the simplest form of a frown, smile, or look of concern.

The Coast Guard teaches their recruits to make sure they're aware of their surroundings and to observe all members of their team at all times. They teach them to:

- Be alert for deviations from standard procedures
- Watch for changes in the performance of other team members
- Be proactive, provide information in advance

- Identify problems in a timely manner
- Show you're aware of what's going on around you
- Communicate effectively

This could be the playbook for teamwork in corporate America. Think about how effective your team would be if they followed the Coast Guard's basic rules for maintaining situational awareness!

In life and in business keep *your* "space radar" up and maintain your situational awareness. You'll find yourself in the catbird seat... knowing, or at the very least, anticipating, and being prepared for what's going to happen next.

Trust but Verify

"Trust, but verify."

This is the phrase that I regularly hear from my mother-in-law, Adrienne Oeding. She's managed a high-end boutique gift shop for some 20 years in Memphis, and I can tell you that she really knows her stuff.

Her mantra is an old Russian proverb made famous by Ronald Regan during the second half of the Cold War. Regan was referring to the extensive verification procedures that would enable the United States and Russia to monitor compliance with a nuclear arms treaty.

My mother-in-law uses the phrase because of how well it pertains to retail business transactions. Trust is a funny thing in our field… and it's a critical component of all business relationships.

Below is some of my favorite advice for building trust in your career …

Stronger Than Oak

One of my favorite movies is *Jerry McGuire*. We all feel Jerry's pain when he's betrayed by his player who abruptly changes sports agents even after his father shakes on a promise and tells Jerry his word is "…stronger than oak." Most people mean what they say and have great intentions, but circumstances can change quickly. People will make choices based on their own self-interest — no matter what they've promised. I've been betrayed in business and now take serious steps to avoid it by documenting my communications with clients and checking in regularly to make sure we're both on the very same page.

Out On a Limb

Ernest Hemingway said it beautifully: "The best way to learn if you can trust somebody is to trust them." It may be tough to believe, but sometimes you have to let go and trust people. To do this, I have a rule of thumb – give a person two times to "prove" him or herself. If they let me down that second time then I know I should keep the relationship at arm's length. However, if they stay consistent and come through, I know it's okay to feel safe.

Example is Powerful

Have you ever been with a client or co-worker who behaves differently around you compared to his or her other relationships? When you see this happen you know two things. First, they're more comfortable around you. Second, they're going to behave differently when you're not around. Until you have a long-standing relationship with a client or customer, be guarded with your words and behavior. Don't bleed the lines between a new relationship and someone you've known for several years. At least not yet!

Awareness

"Situational awareness" is a military term I heard for the first time just a few years ago. It simply means being aware of what's going on around you at all times. I love this term and I urge you to get some – fast. In fact, you'll often hear me use the term with my family in the car…or when someone cuts me off at the store…or when someone is paying more attention to their phone than what they should be doing. It's my biggest pet peeve!

Having a keen sense of your surroundings, particularly in business dealings, will help you see when things might not being going as planned. It may also help you realize when your trust has been compromised. It's that "gut feeling" and honestly, it's usually spot-on.

Don't wait until tomorrow; make sure trust is truly woven into the fabric of your business today. I promise that by making trust a priority in your business you'll rarely find yourself stuck with a Jerry McGuire-esque living room handshake!

Who are your Trusted Advisors?

Some of the most rewarding times I have spent as a leader and a business person were the 3 years I served as the board chair of the Make-A-Wish Foundation of Middle Tennessee. I was nominated to lead the board after having served for only two years, and my first instinct was to seek out advice and experience sharing from someone I trusted and that had served in a similar capacity.

I met with a friend and business associate that was board chair of a large non-profit in Nashville and he gave me two of the best pieces of advice that I still carry with me today. First, he mentioned that when raising funds or in program development, to always lead with the mission of your organization. This would ensure that donors and volunteers never lose sight of what you are trying to accomplish. He also said that it was very important to have "FOB's" on the board. Puzzled at first, I said "FOB's?" Yes, Friends of Ben. Simply put, he meant that for the organization to be successful, I had to have a strong board with people that I trust and vice versa.

I took this experience share to heart and recruited a very strong and trustworthy executive committee with different backgrounds: law, marketing, human resources and finance – my trusted advisors...my FOB's.

Who are the trusted advisors in your life and business? These are the folks that you go to for counsel, advice and guidance when opportunities arise or maybe when things are getting tough. Here are some thoughts on selecting and utilizing those key people in your life.

Circle of Trust

Thomas Moore said, "We need people in our lives with whom we can be as open as possible. To have real conversations with people may seem like such a simple, obvious suggestion, but it involves courage and risk." I love the scene in *Meet the Parents* where Robert DeNiro explains the circle of trust to Ben Stiller. Think of these trusted advisors as your own little circle of trust. I've found that over time, people change, and sometimes not for the better, the circle becomes smaller – so choose wisely.

Key Characteristics

When selecting your trusted advisors keep these characteristics in mind:

Experience: Do they have the experience and tenure to give you the advice and guidance you will need? Do they have experience in your industry or occupation?

Loyalty: One of my favorite quotes is by Joe Mehl "The only people I owe my loyalty to is those who never made me question theirs" Loyalty is especially important in tough times – when true colors in relationships sometimes show through.

Honesty: I recently had a friend give me some honest feedback… it stung a little, but was true. If you can't count on your trusted advisors to be honest, whether the feedback is positive or constructive in nature, it will be difficult to grow and learn.

Diversity

At a leadership meeting recently, our speaker, Consultant Scott Hoesman of *in*QUEST, put the group through an exercise that I thought was very revealing. He had us list our trusted advisors or "go to" network as he called them and then determine if they fit in the following categories:

- Within +/- 10 years of our age
- The same gender, ethnicity or disabled
- Same industry, work experience or location

I found that some of my advisors lacked the characteristics above, proving that the more diverse your trusted advisors are, the different perspectives you will get when seeking advice. It was eye opening.

So, make sure you have your own FOB's in your life and career… and choose wisely…you never know when you'll need them.

TECHNOLOGY – YOUR FRIEND OR FOE?

Take a Break from Technology

Last week, I was with a close friend and client when she mentioned that she'd recently taken a vacation to get out of town but with all her client's needs, emails, and texts, she felt guilty for even leaving. In the end, she never really got the rest and relaxation she needed.

What my friend experienced has become the norm in American business. Vacation is nonexistent, time off generally means time off with access to email, texts and work. In fact, who can't relate when I say that vacation is often spent trying to find a WIFI signal?

I was recently with a group of close friends and colleagues to attend a birthday celebration. I immediately noticed that everyone was on their laptop, cell phone, or tablet checking email, on a conference call or responding to messages they felt were urgent.

So, when do we really un-plug and relax? Never? That's simply not healthy.

In fact, it's not just your customers and clients who will feel the pain when you don't take a break, it'll be your family and friends. So take a moment to read a few suggestions which might help you unplug, unwind and re-charge *YOUR* batteries:

Ding! You Are Free To Move About Your Business

Some of the best times I've had to reflect on my personal life and business are on a plane. Ever have that flight where you thought you'd fall asleep? What else are you going to do...watch some Harry Potter movie and fight for pretzels with your neighbor?

The only time I have 2-4 hours by myself with no distractions is on a plane flight. I manage to decompress, think about my clients and their needs, and at the same time look at what I'm trying to accomplish in the next 6 months. Case in point: I'm writing this article right now from seat 7A on a Southwest flight.

Cell Phone

Simple rules to keep the phone in check:

- take a deep breath…and leave your phone in the car during an important meeting
- if you are going to take your device in to a meeting (maybe to use the calculator as I sometimes do) ALWAYS set to silent or vibrate
- don't take technology to bed, it's not your partner, so don't treat it like one – leave in the kitchen charging

Business at Home and on Vacation

Everyone has a laptop or computer in the kitchen or home office. How often are you working and is it distracting from your family? If the answers are "constantly" and "yes!"…then try these ideas:

- Step outside…literally. Take a minute and if you are working at home, step outside and take a deep breath. Most folks are tied to their laptop or desktop, so take some time to enjoy the reason you are working so hard. You will be amazed at what a short walk will do for you.
- Create set times to work on business issues – after the kids go to bed or early morning before everyone is up. This goes for vacation too – we all know we have to check in now and then, but don't let it dominate your time off. Check your messages in the morning and then let go.
- Let your clients know you will be gone. Taking the right steps BEFORE you leave will insure a relaxing vacation. For years I would feel guilty for being on vacation. Set your "out of office" and let go…you earned it!

So, grab a hold of technology before it takes over you. Step back, un-plug and watch how your "time-out" will actually make you more productive, efficient and at the same time...ready to take on whatever your business and modern technology throws at you.

Steal The Google Playbook

There are only two ways to get a tour of the Google headquarters in Mountain View, California. You have to work at Google or know someone who works there that will kindly take you on a site visit. (Okay, there are really three – be a celebrity and you get access!) Recently, I was fortunate enough to be a guest at the Google campus along with a group of friends, spending the morning on site. I watched closely and learned a lot in the short time I spent there. Here are some take-a-ways from the Google playbook that should translate well into your everyday business life.

Transparency

Although I didn't personally see founders Larry and Sergey, I was told they are very visible and actually attend an "all hands" meeting on a weekly basis to update employees about product and company developments. They even field questions and listen to employee suggestions. How transparent are you with your employees? It was apparent to me that acompany culture promoting open communication and soliciting feedback is going to produce employees that are more productive and motivated.

Health and Community

We started our day at breakfast in one of the main dining rooms.(If you haven't seen the movie "The Internship" then check it out... Vince Vaughn's character finds out quickly that Google provides free meals for all their employees.) What I learned was two things: instead of employees leaving campus for meals – they stay at work and congregate at large community tables and talk to each other! I also observed the wide selection of healthy foods available – M&Ms were in large opaque containers and fruit and granola were in clear, visible bowls – giving the employee a choice. It seemed that they were making the healthier option an easier find. Healthy employee, healthy company.

Creativity

Google oozes with creativity – our friend that gave us our tour said the best part of his job is that no idea is off limits – no product is too crazy, no thought or new idea suppressed. This was very evident in the video, Google Map cars, and prototype airplanes on display throughout the buildings. Just think if every one of your employees said the same about their job at your company…where would your stock price be!?

Earth and Environment

Everywhere we turned at Google there were recycling and compost bins…and Google boasts 1.9 MW of solar panels that produce over 3 million of kWh of clean energy. The electric cars and bicycles reduce their carbon footprint and their investment in renewable energy and green products for customers makes Google one of the greenest companies in America. They are proving it's not easy, but achievable.

Trust and Security

Google empowers their employees with a tremendous amount of trust. We saw first-hand the brightly colored bicycles and electric cars for employees to use to get from building to building and from meeting to meeting. At the same time this trusting and welcoming company was ultra-secure – and they have to be. Outside of check-ing in at the arrival of our visit we were asked several times who our employee-host was and show our credentials. Security cameras were abound – proving that a happy, trusting work environment can be a safe one too.

I had a great experience at Google (I mean, even I want to apply for "The Internship.") Use some of these creative take-aways from the Google playbook to motivate your employees and watch your productivity soar.

Insure to Be Sure

I never thought I would work in the insurance business, let alone for 24 years. When I was in high school and college – I knew I wanted to be in marketing or sales, and work with people. My grandfather worked for State Farm his whole career, but never pushed me or suggested that I follow his path. I've had several titles and responsibilities over the past 24 years…Consultant, Senior Sales Manager, Employee Benefits Representative, Senior Vice President, Managing Director…but at the end of the day, I help friends and clients protect themselves and their companies from the expected…and unexpected…it's called managing risk. It's definitely not sexy, but it is so *very* important. Most people don't realize a need for certain insurance protection until it's too late. I've dealt with too many folks that come to me for help and it's too late as a loss or medical condition has occurred. Here are a couple of products that have changed over the years, but are more important (and less expensive) than ever.

Disability Insurance

The Affordable Care Act or Obamacare as it is widely known has consumed the media and our focus as business professionals and consumers. Unfortunately, other important employee benefits and insurance coverage's are being put on the back burner, but are as important as healthcare – disability insurance is one of those benefits.

Working Americans often assume that either their employer's plan or Social Security will pay an adequate benefit should a disability occur. Over time, I have dealt with three executives, stricken with career-ending disabilities, who each found out too late that they were under-insured, or not insured for disability coverage.

In working with employers, I find that one of the most over-looked employee benefits is long term disability coverage. This all said, it is important for you as a consumer and employee to research your company's program. If they offer a plan, look for the following features to ensure adequate coverage:

- Make sure that the policy covers all sources of income (bonuses and commissions) and that you are covered for your full salary.

- Most plans only cover 60% of income and it is taxable, so consider a supplemental individual policy to cover taxes and shortfalls your employer's plan might have.

- Confirm the plan will pay to age 67 or normal retirement

- Ensure the plans "definition of disability" will cover you in your current occupation, as some policies will pay for a defined period of time, but if you can earn a living elsewhere (even if it is for less money), benefits will cease.

Life Insurance

Thirty years ago, life insurance was sold across the kitchen table by independent agents. Today, most Americans purchase life insurance through payroll deduction with their employer or through an association plan like AAA. Unlike gasoline, groceries, and real estate, life insurance is one of the few consumer products that as actually *decreased* in price. Term Life insurance rates have dropped due to increased life expectancy (we are living longer), health and wellness options available to consumers and the advancement of pharmaceuticals and modern medicine, but still is an overlooked insurance need.

Product features on life insurance have progressed as well, for instance:

- Living Benefits are now a commonplace that allows policy-holders to take life proceeds when diagnosed with a terminal illness

- Employee Assistance Plans, will preparation and emergency travel assistance benefits will often accompany your employer's group life plan

If you haven't reviewed your life plans recently, again, start with your employer and see what coverage you have and consider supplementing your employer's plan with a policy for you, your spouse and children. Most life insurance companies have great calculators online where you can input basic personal information and determine what amount of life insurance you need.

Make sure you take time to review some of the insurance coverage that is most critical to you and your family...insure to be sure, manage your risk...it's not sexy, but very important, especially when you need it most...when you least expect it.

You're Late... You're Forgotten

I was at the airport recently with a group of close friends and we were all on the same flight – and same text thread. Banter ensued back and forth about the upcoming weekend and where everyone was in the airport – some of us were grabbing coffee, some were at the gate and a few still in line at security. My friend looked at me and said "What did we ever do before cell phones?"

I thought for a minute and told him: "We all showed up at the gate early and on time."

Time is a funny thing – as much as technology has enabled us to be more efficient and work smarter, it's made us sloppy in some of the areas of business that are most important – like being on time.

Woody Allen said "80 percent of life is just showing up." I'd argue that 80 percent of life is just showing up...ON TIME! Here are a few ideas to help you manage time, utilize technology, and impress your clients at the same time.

On Time or Out of Sight

Everyone has a client or friend that's habitually late for everything and, unfortunately, it defines them. My friends and I will say we're on "John time" or "Susan time" because we're standing around waiting on them to show up! I was told early on in my career that we have little control over certain details of a meeting or outcome of a sales presentation with the exception of one thing: being on time for the appointment. Be on time or be forgotten.

Send a Message

Sometimes we can't avoid traffic jams or a flat tire. Make sure to use technology to your advantage and let your appointment know you're running late – they'll understand and appreciate the heads up. One of our most valued clients was on her way to our office for a meeting recently and I got a text that read: "Just got rear-ended and waiting for the police to show up." That's not a problem in my book – it was unavoidable. We quickly rescheduled and easily moved forward.

15 Seconds

When I was an insurance rookie I was meeting with one of our largest customers and he said to me "Ben, one of the biggest mistakes people make is not returning phone calls in timely manner… it takes 15 seconds to return a phone call, so just do it!" When did we all become so busy that we had to avoid a call from a close friend or client, or simply not return one? Technology has allowed us to become sloppy. I recently read that Millennials would rather text than listen to a voicemail or return a call. In certain personal communications this might work, but in business – take the 15 seconds.

Set an Alarm

More often than not, we are late because we are busy and lose track of time and then fall behind. Again, utilize technology. Set the alarm on your phone, your Outlook or Google Calendar for important calls or meetings – ensuring you a head start on leaving or being there on time.

R-E-S-P-E-C-T

Keep in mind that tardiness is disrespectful. Plain and simple. You're rarely going to show up at your kid's ball game, family reunion or NFL game late – so why would you dream of being late for a business meeting? Being early gives you the ability to collect your thoughts, check email and messages and…prepare! Show your clients some respect – don't be late.

So for your next big meeting, show up when you say you will and use technology to communicate effectively if you find yourself in an unavoidable situation. Technology is no excuse for sloppiness in business. Be on time or be forgotten!

FAMILY AND PHILANTHROPY

The $40 Glass of Lemonade

I will never forget the most expensive glass of lemonade that I ever purchased. You might think that it was at a beautiful resort on some tropical island, but it wasn't. It was on the tenth hole at a Make-a-Wish Foundation golf tournament in 1995. A young boy named Danny sold me the lemonade. Danny wasn't raising money so that *his* wish could be granted; his had already occurred (he went to Disney World with his family). No, Danny was raising money so that *other* kids could have the same experience he did. That was the day that I spent $40 on a glass of lemonade. That was also the day that I knew I wanted to give back to my community.

I remember thinking, if this 8-year-old boy with a life-threatening illness could give back, why couldn't I? Today, you see more and more kids like Danny. They are forgoing birthday parties and presents, and are having friends bring items for food banks or other donations. Kids are organizing walks, food drives and bake sales to raise money for a charity of their choice. These kids can be role models for us as business leaders in our respective communities.

One of my favorite quotes is by Danny Thomas, founder of St. Jude's Children's Research Hospital: "Success has nothing to do with what you gain in life or accomplish for yourself. It's what you do for others." I love this quote because it really should be about how we define ourselves as business leaders. I have always tried to incorporate giving back to the community by interweaving that goal in my business practices, while including my clients and friends in the process. Here are some ways you and your company can make a meaningful impact with a local charity:

Organize an Employee-Giving or Corporate-Matching Program

This is commonplace at *Fortune 500* companies, but it's easy to do in any size company. Allow your employees to give back through payroll deductions to a charity of their choice. The United Way has a great program for workplace giving, and they also allow your employees to choose where the money goes. If an employee makes a donation outside your corporate giving program, match it up to a certain amount.

Turn Your Holiday Parties and Celebrations into a Philanthropic Team-Building Project

Celebrations and parties are great, but how much better would your employees feel and how much more fulfilling would it be if you spent the same time and money cleaning up a park, building a home with Habitat for Humanity or donating food to Second Harvest Food Bank?

Instead of Birthday or Holiday Gifts for Clients, Make a Donation to a Charity in their Honor

Most holiday or "thank you" gifts get lost in the shuffle of the season. Who remembers the tin of popcorn and where it came from? A handwritten note and a donation in the clients' honor will go a long way. This can be done for birthdays, anniversaries and also in sympathy. Most charities will even send a formal recognition for gifts of more than $25.

Incorporate Charitable Giving as Part of Your Company's Recognition Program

If you have an "Employee of the Month" program or offer service awards based on tenure, incorporate a donation to a charity of way to recognize a valued employee and team member and allow them to their choice. It's a great honor a cause close to their heart.

Organize Teams to Participate in Local Walks, Races or Sporting Events

A fun way to initiate corporate giving *and* wellness is to challenge your employees to enter teams in local 5k races, charity walks or softball tournaments. Most events now have corporate team categories and challenges.

Remember, it's easy to give back to the community while being a successful businessperson. A good friend of mine always says, "It is amazing what you can accomplish when you get a group of people that truly care." Does this define you, your employees and your business? It should.

Handwritten Notes

When was the last time you received a hand written thank you note in the mail from a friend or client? I bet you that you can tell me exactly when you received it, who it was from and why they sent it. Do you know why? In today's world of emails, voicemails, text messages and instant messages, the path of least resistance is to thank someone electronically or not thank them at all.

I remember vividly my childhood and the month of December. My birthday is December 14th and with it being so close to the holidays I would try and get away with thanking grandparents and other relatives with one note for birthday and Christmas gifts.

However, my mom made me sit down on the evening of the 15th and pound out all my thank you notes for my birthday gifts and the same occurred two weeks later after the holidays.

I now want to thank my mom formally for instilling in me the value of thanking someone with a note. It is a lost art. I think we have forgotten how much a nice note means to someone. On several occasions I have walked into the office or home of a friend or client that I have written a note of congratulations or thanks to and the note is pinned to the wall or on their fridge (even weeks or months later). I have even had people call me as soon as they receive my note to let me know how much it meant to them. Recently, I dropped a note and a related business article in the mail to a large prospect. Two weeks later she called and asked me if I could help her with a project – I know my note and article jogged her memory about my company and services. So why don't we take the time to do it...?

I have interviewed hundreds of people in my career and it is amazing how few people take the time to write a thank you note to me for my time. Most interview preparation books and manuals will tell you the last rule of interviewing is make sure you send a handwritten thank you note. The problem with sending an email thank you in today's world is you never know who is reading or checking the person's email. It could be an assistant, trainee, or more that one person could have access to that person's email.

My grandfather, in his retirement, sat with his coffee every morning and wrote in his journal about the prior day's events. He also periodically wrote letters to his children and grandchildren about his travels or a special memory, even after he had mastered the internet. I still have the note he wrote to me the week before I got married. Remember, a note to a friend or client doesn't always have to be a special occasion. Some the best notes I have received were ones just to say "Hello."

There are several reasons to sit down and write a note:

- Nice to meet you!
- Thank you for the business!
- Birthdays, Holidays, Anniversaries, Sympathy.
- "Thank you" for all you do!
- Reminders of important products or ideas.
- Congratulations on …!
- Send a business related or recent article.
- Just to say "Hello."

Greg Hatcher in his book "*55 Steps to Outrageous Service*" explains that writing a simple thank you note accomplishes three things:

1. The person receiving the note feels very good about it.

2. We feel good for having written the note.

3. The person receiving the note becomes a friend and an ally who will help us even more in the future.

As an entrepreneur and business owner, I've always made it a habit at the end of my business week to take a few minutes and review the past week and drop a few notes in the mail, warranted or not. I will also cut out clippings or articles of interest and send with a note to friends or clients. I recently sent a short note and recommendation letter to a client that had lost her job – and stayed in touch with her over the several weeks of her job search. That client landed at a new company and I was the first vendor she brought in to do business at the new company – my note and recommendation letter meant so much to her. All my clients appreciate (and even look forward) to my note and birthday card that I send out every year. So maybe it is time to dust off those note cards and old stationery and think about your really important clients, friends, and relatives…and write them a note of thanks. There's a good chance they'll stick it on their wall or fridge. And just think, it's quite possible that e-mailed thank you note you sent last year is still sitting in their SPAM folder – unopened.

Set an Example for Your Peers

Read the news lately? I'm guessing you scanned several stories about public figures either recently arrested or embroiled in some type of salacious scandal.

And then there's my friend, Kevin Carter. This particular celebrity played 14 seasons in the NFL, works with ESPN, and strives daily to set an incredible example for his community, family, and peers. Spend some time with him and you'll always hear him say, "To whom much is given, much is expected." Carter raised over $1 million for the Make-A-Wish Foundation of Middle Tennessee and The Kevin Carter Foundation over the past 14 years.

Are you wasting your time with frivolous behavior? Or, are you setting a true example for your team? Keep Carter's motto in mind, and start with these simple strategies:

Do the Right Thing

How many times in a week are you faced with an ethical or moral decision, whether it's large or small?

My team recently dealt with some inaccurate information on an application. Whether it was a mistake or intentional, we knew we could not submit the information as is. As tough as that phone call was to the client, we had to make sure the information we had was accurate.

Trust your gut feeling and even though sometimes the right thing is the toughest, it's the best one in the long run. Your team and co-workers are watching you.

It Starts at the Top

I often say that the office runs at the speed of the boss. Everyone that works with you or for you is going to look at how you operate and set his or her day or week at your pace. Make sure you set the right example for your team. I would tell my sales reps to plan their day or week as if the CEO of the company was going to be shadowing them all week. Think about it...how much more productive would you be? I'd bet it's a lot.

Keep Your Eye on the Customer

The way YOU diffuse any customer service problem with a client is likely to be replicated by your team. I've seen vendors lose clients because they treat a prospect better than a current customer. Make sure you have a plan in place to monitor current clients so problems don't fester while you're working with potential customers. Your team will appreciate you being proactive because they don't want to lose a customer any more than you do – they just need the direction to do it.

Continue to Learn and Grow

Great teams that want to blossom must be the most knowledgeable in their industry. Make sure you set an example for your team by continuing your own education. Then, make sure they have tools to learn and grow so that all of you can respond to the current fast-paced business environment.

Jump on the Grenade

No one wants to work for or with someone who delegates away tough situations. When things get rough (and they often do!) be on the front lines with your team. Show that you care, that you're not afraid to roll up your sleeves and get things done.

I vividly remember one of my first high school jobs working at a shoe store. When a customer would get upset, my manager would go hide in his office, leaving the rest of us to deal with heated situations. That's poor management behavior. Instead, stick around and support your team.

So, forget about all those ridiculous celebrity stories. Take your leadership cues from a person like Kevin Carter: never stop setting a great example for your business, and for your peers.

Jay DeMarcus, Kevin Carter, Beth Torres and
Ben Hanback at The Kevin Carter Foundation
Waiting For Wishes Event in Nashville

Take Business Principles Home

Michael J. Fox has it right.

"Family is not an important thing," he said. "It's everything."

There are plenty of successful businesspeople that have families keeping them on the right track. How you "work" with your family is just important as your day-to-day job. Here are a few solid business principles that can be woven into your family life every day:

Respect

Imagine if your biggest client walked in to your office and you started to rifle through your mail. I'd bet they wouldn't be your client for very long. How many times have you done the exact same thing at home after a long day a work, forgetting to acknowledge your family first? If you wouldn't do it at work, certainly don't make it a habit at home. Make sure you greet your family like you would a client. Respect goes a long way.

Goals

In my entrepreneur organization, not only do we focus on business goals, but we also take time to put together "Family Goals and Planning." This has always highlight what we hoped to accomplish on a personal level – attending more of your children's events, budgeting, home projects, vacations ... we even take a look at relationships with friends and family that may need some attention. Like any solid business goal, review your personal goals on a regular basis and adjust when necessary.

Meetings

Back when I started my own company in 2007, my wife and I created a standing lunch "date" every Friday afternoon. We both bring our calendars and discuss the week ahead. We plan everything from vacations to dentist appointments to kid's activities. Like a good business meeting, we make sure we stay focused on the priorities of our family unit. Our Friday times together ensure that we never look at each other and exclaim, "You never told me about this!" Instead, we meet and plan accordingly.

Communication and Feedback

Successful organizations will do surveys on a frequent basis, gauging customer needs and then tweaking their goals and business plans. When was the last time you surveyed your own family?

We try and include our kids in most important family decisions like vacations, sports activities, weekend plans, and meals. Then, we get feedback on how things are going. For example, we love movies and have a "Tuesday Movie Night" with our kids every week. We take turns choosing the flick. We've found that if we get feedback from the kids on what we're watching – or the things we're doing – there's little to complain about down the road. My wife, kids, and I are all happy customers.

Phones and Computers

I'll admit it. I'm at the kitchen table with my laptop as I write this article. No family is perfect, but we are trying to get better about putting away our phones away at dinner or family gatherings. Just like that annoying cell phone ring during a business meeting, unplug every once and a while so that you can spend uninterrupted time with those who are most important to you.

"I believe that being successful means having a balance of success stories across the many areas of your life," said one of my favorites,

Zig Ziglar. "You can't truly be considered successful in your business life if your home life is in shambles."

Trust Alex P. Keaton and Zig Ziglar. When you're climbing the corporate ladder you want to make sure your loved ones aren't left too far behind.

Brittany Hanback, Campbell Hanback, Ben Hanback and Bella Hanback at U2's concert in Boston, MA

LEADERSHIP
AND
PERSONAL
DEVELOPMENT

After You Know It All...

A close friend recently shared a quote with me from legendary basketball coach John Wooden, "What really counts in life is what you learn after you know it all."

I laughed and then thought for a moment about a business situation I was currently handling where I couldn't stop digging my heels in the ground. I was simply refusing to adjust my way of thinking. And, right then, Coach Wooden's words hit home.

As technology and business change so quickly, this quote has never been more relevant. I remember when I first started my career and we were manually calculating insurance rates and pricing. I was on a committee at my old company to determine whether or not it would make sense to roll out handheld devices (remember the Palm Pilot?) for our sales reps. Not only is Coach Wooden speaking about growing and learning, but he's also talking about flexibility and change. With the New Year upon us, here are a few ideas and areas that can help you start fresh once *YOU* know it all:

Personal Development

I've always tried to keep personal development as a part of my business growth – whether it was a class on public speaking, reading the hottest business book, or an industry specific class or seminar. Now it's easier than ever to take advantage of these opportunities. My 15-year old daughter of all people introduced me to TED Talks. Now, I love watching them and choosing topics related to sales or relationship building. Make sure you have a personal development plan woven in to your business goals – it's an easy way to keep current, grow, and learn.

Humility

Coach Rick Pitino said, "Humility is the true key to success... Humble people share the credit and wealth, remaining focused and hungry to continue the journey of success." Choose to be humble – it is an incredibly important characteristic to have when you're in business. Someone once told me that humility includes the following: respecting others and their opinion; listening more, speaking less; withholding judgment; sharing credit, helping and promoting others.

We probably all could use a dose of humility from time to time – so keep it in mind when dealing with your co-workers, teammates, friends, and family.

Hard Work and Respect

Throughout my career, I've never run into a business problem or situation that couldn't have been prevented or solved if everyone involved in the situation had simply worked hard and respected one another – it's amazing what hard work will accomplish. Talk to your staff regularly about giving 100 percent and showing mutual respect to one another. With this in mind, the journey will be smoother and the accomplishment well-earned.

Don't Forget Where You Came From

Just as important as growing and learning is … so is making sure you share with your team and co-workers what made you successful. And, as quickly as things change there are business ideas, traits, and practices that will never become obsolete. I recently spoke to a group of young leaders volunteering with Make-A-Wish of Middle Tennessee. I was asked to share the history of our chapter and the successes (and struggles) we had over the past 15 years. As important as it is to look forward and embrace change, under-standing and learning from those that have already walked that walk is equally important.

So, in life and business – and once YOU know it all – remember to keep working hard, continue learning, show respect to others, and stay humble. Then continue down *YOUR* path of success!

Attitude is a Choice

I've found that there are a couple basic types of people out there.

There's the kind who sucks the energy out of the atmosphere with a gloomy outlook and facial expressions (*think "Debbie Downer"*), and then there's another kind who rarely appears to be in a bad mood – they lift the spirits of anyone they meet. Look closely at the difference between the attitudes -- which one best describes someone you'd want to do business with?

If you selected the second description, then you've chosen wisely. How you approach a situation should never be haphazard, it should be a conscious decision you make each day.

Be that uplifting person by employing some of these simple tips. Then watch your relationships grow.

Let it Go

Ever since I was a teenager, my father would tell me not to waste time on things I had no control over. This statement was both a life lesson AND a business lesson. Too many people spend valuable time fretting over situations or outcomes they can't control. For example, I've watched sales people worry and waste time after they've made a presentation. Even if you did everything perfect, the outcome will always be out of your control. Keep a positive attitude and move onto more productive tasks.

Reframe the Issue

One of my favorite quotes on attitude is from Olympic Gold Medalist Scott Hamilton who said: "The only disability in life is a bad attitude." After eight long years of trying to start a family, my wife and I found out we weren't able to have children naturally. Devastated at the time, our doctor asked us this simple question: "Do you want to have a baby or do you two want to be parents?" With the turn of a phrase he changed our outlook and attitude towards parenting. We began pursuing adoption and today we have two beautiful children.

Humor For the Win

An edgy, tension-filled room is not uncommon in today's business world. I often break the ice with a joke or a (tasteful!) funny comment. There's nothing wrong with injecting some fun and laughter into stressful situations. It's amazing how attitudes will immediately improve with a smile and a laugh. Humor will often force folks be more receptive to your product, ideas, or presentation.

Don't Overlook an Opportunity

Many business people are shortsighted – they've made their minds up that there's a perfect customer or client. You may not want to waste your time with high maintenance clients, but having the right attitude and outlook with newer customers and prospects can pay off in the long run. Some of my oldest and closest clients started out as small companies. Some were even people that no one wanted to work with. If you can look beyond the immediate hurdles and see the potential of that company down the road, it can pay off big time.

Be Real and Power Through

When our first child arrived, a friend shared some great advice with me. He told me that my son might fall off his bike and get sick now and again, but that at the end of the day it was my attitude and how I *handled* situations that would truly determine the outcome. I've seen people fall apart during moments that may seem serious but are, in reality, quite manageable. My dear friend, Kim, is currently battling breast cancer. I've learned multitudes from her positive outlook and bold attitude. She sets an example for her family and friends. Even on her worst days, she's still at her best. And, that's a lesson in strength for each of us.

Remember, you have the capacity to choose your attitude and impact others each day. Make the decision to choose wisely!

Business Etiquette

On a client call recently, I had to take an elevator up to the top of a building for my scheduled appointment. While lurching up floor by floor, a few things happened in that small space that really made me reflect on how etiquette has virtually vanished in today's business world.

First, two of the people on the elevator proceeded to discuss a co-worker's personal problems and someone was having a personal conversation on their cell phone. Second, when the elevator door opened up, two people stormed in without letting the three people out that were getting off.

Now before you roll your eyes and call me "old school," think about this – when was the last time you were in a meeting or presentation and at least one cell phone didn't ring? Or when was your inbox not full of junk or chain emails?

I was at a conference on the topic of workplace stress and the speaker asked everyone in the room (there were probably 200 attendees) to turn their cell phones up to the "loud" position. You can imagine what happened – over the next five minutes, the room was full of ringers and songs. His point was how stressful today's work environment is, and he easily proved the importance of turning off cell phones during a business meeting.

So what's happened to business etiquette in today's business casual – email –text-messaging world? Here are some rules of thumb to keep in mind as you conduct your business and run your company:

Business Dress

My college coach always used to say: "You've got to look good getting off the bus." This is still true and it's especially true with first impressions. People want to work with sharp, professional individuals. Even if you're in a more casual industry such as the IT or the music business, you can still present yourself well.

- Stay away from artificial flavors – no heavy cologne or perfume.

- Avoid flashy jewelry or sports watches with business dress.

- If ever in doubt of attire, remember, it's better to be overdressed.

- Update your wardrobe periodically to stay current with changing styles or trends.

Phone and Fax

I love my iPhone and do more business on it than the land line, but everyone has to be reminded of some simple rules:

- Return phone calls by the end of the day – no excuse.

- ALWAYS ask before you put someone on hold and never put someone on hold if you initiated the phone call.

- Make sure to include a fax cover page and call ahead before you send a fax over six pages.

- Leave your cell phone in the car…don't even think about taking it in to important meetings. This leaves no room for error – if you have to have it, set it to silent.

- You should never leave a voicemail much longer than a minute or so and always leave your callback number at the beginning and end of the message.

- If putting someone on speakerphone, always announce who's in the room before the conversation starts.

Email

Email is not formal like a written letter and email doesn't disappear when it's deleted. Email can make you feel like there's a bond when there isn't and should never be used for sensitive messages.

- Respond to emails by the end of the day or at worst 24 hours, if it is going to be longer, make sure you have your out of office messenger turned on.

- Ask permission before including someone on a distribution list, and if sending an email to a large list, blind copy the recipients (my pet peeve!)

- Always check your address list before hitting send and never forward an off-color or inappropriate email.

- Don't use an email to vent. If you are upset, call the person or save the email and re-read it the next day. Never use all capitals – that's practically screaming in print.

- We all know if you don't forward your silly limerick to 20 friends, you will have bad luck the rest of your life, but we don't care. Never send chain emails to clients, customers or prospects.

So, shine those shoes, save the cologne and perfume for Saturday night, set that cell phone to silent, and get ready to impress your clients.

Comfort Zone

"WHO AM I?! I AM A SPARTAN!" the starter screamed to us as we reluctantly stared at the daunting path ahead. I recently competed with a close group of friends, Keith Rice, Joey Lewis, and Chris and Whitney Morris, in one of the ultra-competitive, grueling adventure races called the *Reebok Spartan Race*. It was a 5 ½ mile "sprint" consisting of off-road running, over 23 obstacles and with the rain, wind and mud, we found ourselves braving the elements of Mother Nature, too. Not knowing what to expect, I went in to the race uncomfortable and very anxious — *definitely* outside *my* comfort zone.

We quickly realized that this race was not for the faint of heart. The obstacles consisted of scaling mud walls, carrying buckets of gravel, concrete spheres, and sandbags…crawling the length of a football field below barbed wire 12 inches over our heads…all in the rain and mud. After the race, we had different perspectives on what we had accomplished, but we all agreed on one thing: ditching our security blankets made us better athletes. Like in competitive sports, stepping outside of your business comfort zone can be a good thing too. Here are the benefits of taking risks and letting go of the familiar.

Reaffirm Strengths

The one thing that was clear from the beginning of the race was that I was surprisingly stronger than I thought when challenged. My training and preparation had paid off and even though difficult, I was able to handle whatever was thrown in front of me. Brian Eno, the legendary producer for the rock band U2, said "People tend to play in their comfort zone, so the best things are achieved in a state of surprise, actually." Make sure as a business professional you realize your strengths, take advantage of where you excel, and use that to your advantage.

Expose Weaknesses

Taking risks and challenging yourself will expose areas of improvement for you and your team. In the *Spartan Race*, I was not as prepared for the running portion of the challenge as I had thought, and found myself taking breaks to catch my breath. I now know where to focus my training.

Professionals will gravitate to what is familiar vs. learning a new skill or product. Step outside your comfort zone and identify your shortfalls so you can take the extra steps needed to improve in those critical areas.

Alternative Perspective

This race was different than a 5k or half-marathon. It forced us to help each other and work as a team. This included everything from emotional encouragement to physical help over a mud wall or rock climb. By stepping outside our area of comfort we realized the finish line was *impossible* without the help of others.

Clear Head & Re-focus

The day after the *Spartan Race*, I was able to clear my thoughts, and re-focus my training. By stepping outside of your business comfort zone, you will be able to reflect on your past accomplishments and shortcomings, and re-focus moving forward. Actor and comedian Chris Rock, who will host this year's Academy Award's has always re-focused his act and career. He mentions that "Comedians tend to find a comfort zone and stay there and do lamer versions of themselves for the rest of their career." Rock has always stayed fresh with performing and it's not by accident.

Risk & Creativity

Finally, escaping familiarity will open your mind and force you to be more creative. This is risky – it's human nature to hover in the status quo. There's story after story of executives and entrepreneurs that "reinvent themselves" mid-career and change focus. This takes a leap of faith as well as creativity. Taylor Swift, who recently changed genres from country to pop talks about one of her idols "One element of Madonna's career that really takes center stage is how many times she's reinvented herself. It's easier to stay in one look, one comfort zone, one musical style. It's inspiring to see someone whose only predictable quality is being unpredictable."

Spartan athletes are stepping outside their comfort zone every weekend, tuning out the noise of modern life and challenging themselves to be stronger, more focused athletes. Stepping outside *YOUR* comfort zone and challenging yourself can ensure that you will be ready for the obstacles that business and life throw in front of you. **WHO ARE YOU?! BE A BUSINESS SPARTAN!**

Ben Hanback competes in the Reebok Spartan Race

Decisions, Decisions

Let's be honest: making choices is not for the faint of heart.

One of my closest friends recently transitioned careers. He confided that it was one of the most important and nerve-wracking times in his life. As with any big shift, he wondered if he was making the right decision. And, for me, his transition hit very close to home.

I decided to branch out and start my own business in 2007. At the time, a trusted business advisor told me he always tries to *"make a decision and make it the right one"*. That stuck with me and it's guided me through the ups and downs. I've learned that confident decision-making is equally important in business and in everyday life.

Here are some ways to tackle those important decisions while leaving the *Tums* in the medicine cabinet:

Trust Your Gut

I love when Charlie Sheen's character Bud Fox quotes Sun-Tzu's *Art of War* in the movie *Wall Street*: "If your enemy is superior, evade him. If angry, irritate him. If equally matched, fight, and if not, split and reevaluate."

Have you ever been in a complicated business situation and that little voice inside your head screams "WTH?" Well, listen up! That little voice is your gut – and 9 times out of 10 it's usually right. When you're facing a big decision, do your homework, but when things don't feel right (and sometimes that's more often than you'd think), back away and re-evaluate. You can thank me (and Bud Fox) later...

Never Look Back

I think everyone has a friend or co-worker that when at restaurants orders…then, without fail, decides they should have chosen something else. They look around the table sheepishly at other people's meals, convinced they made the wrong choice. I have affectionately coined this *"entrée envy"*. These folks should really listen to motivational speaker Tony Robbins when he says: "Stay committed to your decisions, but be flexible in your approach." With any important decision you've already made, be confident because the second you start to question yourself it's all over. Next time – you can try something a little different…but this time, trust yourself.

Get Comfortable Being Uncomfortable

Local Hendersonville native and IndyCar driver, Josef Newgarden, made a decision to take a big risk last Sunday. In the first lap at Barber MotorSports Park in Birmingham, he moved from 5th place to 2nd place in a matter of seconds by throttling down at the drop of the green flag. At the end of the race when most drivers would slow down (for fear of running out of gas,) he believed in his car, his team and his own abilities and won the first IndySeries race of his career.

All great business people have their own horror stories about their own crazy risks or chances taken with a failed outcome. Warren Buffet often talks about investments or companies that cost him too much money. Then there's racecar driver Mario Andretti who once said that if things seem like they're under control then "…you are just not going fast enough." Making decisions to take chances and risks is going to feel uncomfortable. Get used to it. The finish line might just be worth it – just ask Josef.

Chief Distractor

I vividly remember studying for the ACT in high school and my AP English teacher, Mrs. Ruth Dunning, explaining the concept of the "chief distractor" to our class.

In a four question multiple-choice test you have one right answer, two wrong answers and one chief distractor – the answer that seems right and makes you think twice, but it's definitely wrong.

When faced with tough decisions in your daily business life make sure you identify *YOUR* chief distractor. Eliminate it immediately and your decisions will become much clearer. In 2007, mine was choosing between joining a larger firm and starting my own business. I made the right choice.

Business decisions are never easy, but just like Mario Andretti, it's okay to speed up a little...take some risks. And, when you make that big decision, make it the RIGHT one...then never look back.

Happiness in Business

I know you've heard it: Pharrell's mega-hit "Happy," where he effortlessly belts out: "...Because I'm *happy*...clap along if you feel like a room without a roof..."

Now, wouldn't you just love it if that line accurately described your attitude about your business?

Happiness is a funny thing. It comes and goes, and it means something different to everyone. My friend and the successful president of Paramore, Hannah Paramore, always quotes writer Rita Mae Brown who once said, "Happiness is pretty simple – someone to love, something to do, something to look forward to."

Apply this philosophy to your work and I think you'll find yourself in a "Happy" state of mind. Follow these simple steps to get there:

Love What You Do

Our CEO at Make-A-Wish of Middle Tennessee, Beth Torres, finishes every social media post and every email with #bestjobever. She knows she's fortunate to lead a great team and do what she loves: give back and make a difference. Do you love what you do? If you're not sure, then work on loving it. I never thought I'd be in the sales and insurance business but I LOVE meeting new people, connecting relationships, and making new contacts. The best part of my job is meeting community leaders, getting to know companies, and understanding how they grow and prosper. If you aren't doing EXACTLY what you love, work on finding just a slice of what you do love...it will make all the difference.

Something To Do

The worst thing in life and business is sitting idle, especially in today's tech-heavy business world of distractions – from never-ending news-feeds to friends and clients posting their every move on social media. I've seen so many successful people retire early, then realize they're bored and decide to re-enter the business world. Benjamin Franklin once said, "It is the working man who is the happy man. It is the idle man who is the miserable man." I couldn't agree more. Whether you're a CEO or you're in an entry-level position, it's human nature to work hard for that sense of accomplishment. A close friend once told me that when hiring people, you want the folks who don't have to be told how to do things or what to do. They're the people in business that, when faced with a lull, will find a new task, make it meaningful and give them purpose.

Something To Look Forward To

Definitely for myself, and I think most people in business, the best motivator is having something to look forward to – whether it's an accomplishment, a vacation…even a Friday! It's really a very simple way to achieve a goal. I used to set achievable business goals on a three-month basis, but now I focus on just two or three weeks at a time. In this fast-paced business world I have short-term goals that I can look forward to reaching quickly. At the same time, when I have something that I'm REALLY looking forward to, it helps me focus on getting through the daily grind – I know that there's a light at the end of the tunnel. Take that vacation or special Saturday with friends and make it a motivator to accomplish your tasks at hand. You'll have a lot more fun.

Don't waste any more time. Find a way to love what you do, stay busy, and keep your eyes on the prize. I guarantee you'll be singing along with Pharrell at the end of the day!

What's your Pillow Factor?

I had the chance to catch up with my friend and business associate Chris Stout of Evergreen Sports and Entertainment recently. While discussing mutual business opportunities he mentioned that he asks his clients, "What's your pillow factor?" I interrupted him to say I LOVE that...but what exactly does 'pillow factor' mean?

Stout explained that he wants his clients to be comfortable with his advice and decision...so much so that they sleep like a baby every night – a characteristic he calls the "pillow factor." I found that Stout's phrase is not only applicable to financial investment advice, but it also applies to everyday business dealings. How comfortable are you with your decisions in your business and your career? What keeps you up at night? Think about it and then scan my advice for a good day's business and a good night's rest.

Planning

Business planning is essential. In fact, it's so essential that you'll toss and turn if you don't plan properly. I'm a big believer in merging goals with planning, but also keeping things realistic. I advise that you plan every day as if your boss or CEO was going to be shadowing you. How much more productive would you be if they were on your tail? Would you be on surfing the web on business hours? Probably not. If I retained one thing from business school it was that goals have to be attainable, written down, and then reviewed. Make sure you keep your goals within reach, solidify them, and review them on a regular basis.

The "What If?"

Every business has to have a back-up plan. You know that 'oh *NO!'* moment, right? I promise you'll rest easy if you have a plan in place just in case your business was to be rocked by something unexpected. We've all seen a city or town devastated by a hurricane, tornado or flood. What's your flood? How are you going to handle it if it DOES happen? In my entrepreneur organization we did an exercise called just that: *What's your flood?* We planned for the absolute worst thing that could happen to our business and then prepared for it. Try it. Even if the worst never happens, you'll sleep soundly knowing you're ready.

Hard Work

I love the quote by author Jeff Olson, "Successful people do what unsuccessful people are not willing to do." This really says it all. It's the perfect balance of risk and hard work vs. the reward at stake.

Some 23 years ago I was walking out to the parking garage at our office building at 7:30 PM after a long day. My mentor, Brian Dillion, hit me in the arm and said, "look around Benjy, and tell me what cars you see here at almost 8 pm?"

I said, "The expensive ones…Mercedes, BMW, Lexus."

"Exactly," Dillion said. "The successful people are here working the long hours."

That's always stuck with me. You can never replace a hard day's work or extra effort. My friend, Greg Hatcher, often reminds me: "The harder you work the luckier you get." I had the chance to meet ESPN analyst and local resident, Kirk Herbstreit, recently and he mentioned that when he started in broadcasting and still today he was going to be a "grinder" – meaning the hardest working and most knowledgeable broadcaster in the business – it has paid off.

I promise that a hard day's work will not only achieve that "pillow factor," but you'll also get a sense of accomplishment about what most folks may not be willing to do.

Do the Right Thing

We've all done it – held back, remained silent, or turned our head and crossed our fingers in a business situation. By not doing the right thing you're putting you and your business in an "at risk" situation. One of the best ways to sleep soundly at night is to always do the right thing. Although sometimes these are some of the toughest decisions in business, making the ethical choice will give you the most peace of mind in the long run.

Follow these simple steps and not only will you sleep better at night, but your clients and co-workers will too. I promise that achieving your "pillow factor" is contagious...make sure you spread the good word.

ESPN College Football Analyst Kirk Herbstreit and Ben Hanback

Productivity

When I first started my career in sales, our team's focus was productivity – plain and simple. We would say we were going to work *half days*, we just had to figure out which 12 hours it was going to be. How many times at the end of the day or the week do you come up for air and think "What in the world have I accomplished?" Time flies, stress levels are up, and the race to get ahead is faster than ever. Here are some simple ways to keep that stress level down, stay productive, and put yourself ahead of the competition.

Write at Least One Hand-Written Note a Week to Thank a Customer

There is nothing more important than building solid, long-term relationships with your clients. And, there's no simpler way to do that than with a personal note. Most people will tell you they're too busy. Too busy doing what? Come on! It takes two minutes and will have a long-lasting impact. I often will see my notes at people's desk or on their fridge and it means a lot. The average American gets one piece of handwritten mail every *7 WEEKS*... make sure that piece of mail is from *YOU*.

Turn an Unexpected Cancellation into an Opportunity for Long-Term Business Planning

If I retained one thing from business school, it was the rules of goal setting. Those goals must be attainable, written down, and reviewed. An unexpected cancellation can create a perfect space in your schedule to either create or review those goals.

Delegate

Feeling overwhelmed? Ask yourself, *"What's the best use of my time at this very moment?"* You'll find you're doing something that could easily be delegated or postponed. Take advantage of handing over tasks – it could provide you with the space you need to move your business along more productively. If it's a task you can't delegate, then prioritize and save it for later.

Make Your Worst Phone Call by 10 am

No matter what your role is in business, each day brings a phone call or a meeting that no one wants to make or have. Make that phone call early in the day, and you can move ahead with your afternoon. You may even find the call simply wasn't as bad as you feared.

Make the Most of Windshield Time

I vividly remember driving from Memphis to Nashville in 1992 and my manager at the time had cleaned out his desk, loading me up with a stack of business and motivational books on tape for the ride. He said to "make the most of my drive" and stay productive. I popped in the first cassette (remember those?) and the narrator kept mentioning this new technology that will change the way we do business...revolutionary, mind blowing, and speeding up our communication (but wait, I had to flip the cassette to Side Two to see what this game changer was)...the FAX MACHINE. The *fax machine*? I was *already* faxing quotes and proposals. Turns out the cassette tape was a few years old! Regardless of your commute or drive, turn off sports talk and take the extra time in the car to be as productive as possible: catch up on your business and personal phone calls, listen to a *CURRENT* motivational book on CD, or record notes on business planning for future use.

Learn How to Say "NO"

When you're trying to stay productive, unexpected opportunities can quickly turn into distractions, pulling you away from your ultimate business goal. Don't be afraid to say "no." I had an opportunity arise recently and then quickly realized it would take several hours of planning so I said no. I brought my focus back to the work that's absolutely essential to growing my business and profitability.

So, take these tips to heart and not only will you soon be working *half days*, but your productivity will also soar to new heights.

Simple Solutions are Best

Have you heard the old story about the delivery truck that gets stuck under a bridge in a small town? The truck was just too big to clear the small tunnel. So, most of the town gathered around the scene to see what had happened, and to figure out how to free the truck from the small pathway. The town's engineers and businesspeople tried, but couldn't figure out what to do…and then, a small girl – watching the scene with her mother – chimed in. She told the truck driver that if he simply let the air out of his tires, the truck would shrink in height and he'd be able to back up the vehicle. It was simple – and it worked.

In today's world, simplicity goes a long way. Here are some streamlining tips for tackling problems we often struggle with at work and at home:

Meetings

People love to meet. Business people LOVE to have meetings. And so, I put some limits on them: if an issue can be handled in an email or a short conference call, there is no reason to meet. If a meeting is unavoidable, then have an agenda, a time limit, a clear purpose and a defined ending to the meeting. In my Entrepreneur Organization business group we assign what we affectionately call the "TIME NAZI" to make sure everyone keeps his or her portion of the meeting in check. I also advise that you invite ONLY the people that absolutely must be present. In fact, I recently sat through a meeting I should never have been invited to; instead I should have simply received an action item summary.

Presentations

Ever asked a question in a meeting and instead of a concise answer, all you hear is extemporaneous babble? Our Vice President of Marketing, Brian O'Meara, always quotes author Jay Frost: "Be Bright, Be Brief, Be Gone." I love this. If you've ever seen any of the TED Talks online, you'll notice that they are usually 20 minutes or less. They are educational and straight to the point. Too many presentations nowadays contain slide after PowerPoint slide of material that no one reads. Keep your presentations to a photo or an image, and limited talking points. Bring the focus back on you and what you're trying to accomplish. Your audience will thank you – I promise.

Communication

I've been in my industry for a while now and I'd bet we have more acronyms than the military. NBOC is New Business Old Contract …or LTIP is Long-Term Income Protection. What might be commonplace in your world may not be to everyone else, so make sure you always consider your audience. Be transparent in your writing and speech. Don't confuse people when you're talking about a subject you know like the back of your hand. Simplify information for your readers and listeners.

Home Front

Your home life can be just as hectic as your business life. For instance, how many times have you asked your children to complete a task and the first word out of their mouths is, "Why?" It drives me CRAZY! However, when you stop to think about it, they may actually have a point. Today's generation routinely questions *everything* before they execute *anything*. So, try this. Simply explain what you're trying to accomplish before you ask for their help: "Can you go down and open the garage door?" Your child: "Why?" Instead, eliminate extra conversation by first saying, "We're expecting a delivery in 15 minutes, can you help me by running down and opening the garage door?" By helping them understand the purpose and importance of your request, you eliminate confusion. Try it. You'll be pleasantly surprised.

Now go save yourself some valuable time! Simplify your tasks at work and at home, then sit back and enjoy some streamlined success.

Don't Be a Valentine This Year

I have a nickname for a specific New Year's resolution – and only my wife and close friends know what it really means. The name is "Valentine" and I define it as an actual person that makes a resolution at the start of the New Year and usually gives up on it by mid-February

Now, it can be a blast to make a list of resolutions. You can really get a jump on life in the New Year. That's why in December and January television and radio commercials are flooded with weight loss products, including diet pills and exercise machines…and for good reason. Most "Valentines" can be found at health clubs, the local gym or dunking themselves in YMCA swimming pools.

You see, I spend most of my first quarter helping these poor folks find a towel, open their locker, or show them how to use a weight machine. Then by mid-February, they go to dinner with their sweetheart, realize they love them unconditionally and they stop working out.

But not all "Valentines" are found at the local Y.

As an entrepreneur, we tend to plan, set goals, and make resolutions for the new business year, but how many of those goals are followed through and achieved? I once read that it takes 21 days to form – or quit – a habit. That means three weeks to quit smoking, get into a routine of running or working out, or making sure the business plans that are crucial to your success are followed through…week in and week out.

If you haven't taken the time to set goals or plans for the upcoming year, here are six business principles that you can do from here on out:

Prepare Every Business Day as if Your Biggest Client was going to Spend the Day with YOU

How different would your day would be if your number one client was going to shadow you. Would you take an extra 30 minutes at lunch? Would you surf the Internet when you should be following up with important tasks? How much more productive would you be if you planned your week with this in mind? Stop and think about it.

Get Your Worst Call Over With

No matter what your role is in business, each day brings a phone call we don't want to make. It could be to tell a client that their order is not complete, or to tell a vendor that they aren't going to be awarded the business. I've found if you make this phone call early in the day, your day is more productive and usually the call just isn't as bad as you feared. Also – you didn't waste the afternoon worrying about making that call.

Spend 45 Minutes on Personal Development Each Day

Personal development is crucial to and entrepreneur's success. This may be catching up on the Wall Street Journal news rags stacked up behind your desk, reading a trade journal, or studying for a class. Whatever you choose to do for personal development, make sure you set the time aside at the beginning or end of the day to get this in. It will pay out big dividends in the future.

Meet One New Person Each Week

Life is a relationship network and your success in business depends on the relationships you develop. I guarantee you if you practice this principle, your business will blossom.

Write That Thank You Note

There is nothing more important than thanking a client, and no better way to do it than a personal note. Most people will tell you they're too busy to write a note...too busy doing what? It takes two minutes.

Review Your Business Goals on a Weekly Basis

If I retained one thing from business school, it was the rules of setting goals:

- *Goals must be attainable*

- *Goals must be written down*

- *Goals must be reviewed*

If you want your goals to be crystallized in your mind and business practice, you have to review them on a regular basis. Make sure you take the time at the beginning of the week to be sure it includes activities that help you get to your final destination. Sometimes your goals need to be tweaked throughout the year...and you simply won't know that if you don't continue to review them.

So, if you haven't made your personal or business resolutions yet, stop worrying because it's not too late. And if you did, hang in there – the "Valentines" will be gone soon. Just make sure you're not one of them.

Visualization in Business

I was driving my family back from the beach recently and my wife caught me talking to myself (not the first time, of course). She asked me what in the world I was saying. I had to think for a minute, and then realized I was walking through a tough business conversation I had to have the next day...and I was strategically talking through exactly what I was going to say to my client.

As a former college track athlete, I'd often visualize the outcome of an event or imagine how I'd perform. You'll often see placekickers in college football and the NFL do the exact same thing – envisioning the ball go through the uprights with laser concentration before the ball is snapped. My friend Rob Bironas, placekicker for the Tennessee Titans, has told me he sees the ball hit the back of the net before he even kicks.

As business leaders we should take advantage of this sports-related technique. And to prove it, here are four areas where visualization can make an impact on you, your business and your career:

Public Speaking

Studies show that people fear speaking in public first...and death second. Sweaty hands, dry mouth and a pounding chest usually accompany this fear. The old rule of public speaking to "imagine everyone in their underwear" has never worked for me. Instead, I imagine each part of a speech.

I recently spoke to a group of 125 high school students and in preparation for the event I presented the speech to my own children, then imagined the speech going exactly how I wanted it to. I wanted the students to really hear what I had to say and learn from my experience.

If you expect the worst, you may just crash and burn. Think positive...and leave the underwear in the laundry.

Presentations

I love the quote by Coach Vince Lombardi: "Practice does not make perfect, only perfect practice makes perfect." It's relevant to every business presentation out there. The more prepared you are, the more you'll be able to visualize a positive outcome and be prepared for any logistical challenges. Always ask yourself these questions:

"Do I have a back-up copy of my presentation material?"

"Do I have an extra power cord?"

"Do I have plenty of extra paper copies in case unexpected attendees show up or if the technology fails?"

Visualize your presentations at least a week before the big meeting – not on the drive or flight there.

Important Phone Call or Conversation

Just like me talking to myself on the way home from the beach, if it's a call I'm preparing for, I make sure I know exactly what I need to say before I pick up the phone. You need to be clear and concise – never leave room for misunderstanding.

Try visualizing your answers if tough questions are fired at you. How are you going to respond? Exactly what do you want to convey? Know the answers before starting the conversation.

Job Interviews

There's probably not a more important meeting than the one with a potential employer. I love the scene in *Risky Business* when Joel (Tom Cruise) has to think on his feet when the college recruiter shows up at his house. Keep in mind that an interview is about the subject you know best: Yourself.

Most interviewers already know you'll be nervous and anxious, so put them at ease immediately with your confidence. Make sure you have answers for any gaps in your career or employment history, then relax and visualize the meeting as a conversation as opposed to an interview.

I've interviewed hundreds of people and I've found that the more questions they ask me, the more interest they show in the opportunity, and, the more I (the interviewer) am at ease.

So, just like Rob Bironas on Sunday at LP Field, business people are also performing and competing at a high level. Prepare and visualize success every time and you're almost certainly guaranteed a win.

The 1988 Memphis State sprint team L to R Eric Newton, Shannon Banks, Orin Carpenter, Joe Boyland, Ben Hanback, and Norman Reed

BUILDING
YOUR TEAM

Championship Team

With college and pro football in full swing, and with the NBA and NHL about to start, I can't help but think about the parallels between being a championship sports franchise and running a successful business or corporate team.

I was on three different state championship teams growing up, and in business, I've been part of some very successful sales teams and companies. Regardless of the sport or the business, *ALL* great teams have several traits in common.

Great Vision and Motivation

Great teams start with great leadership. Most employees or team members will not only look to managers and leaders for vision, they'll also look for motivation. You'll often hear our bank president, Jim Schmitz, say *"Let's feed the lion while we build the cage."* He means that having sense of urgency in executing a plan is important for long-term vision.

I had the chance to hear Shane Battier talk about his days at Duke, playing for Coach Krzyzewski. He told the story of Coach K comparing his team to a hand and said, "A basketball team is like the five fingers on your hand. If you can get them all together, you have a fist. That's how I want you to play!"

Great leaders surround themselves with a great supporting cast, share their vision, then delegate – and then they trust the folks they have chosen and let them do their jobs. Does this describe how you and your team are operating?

A Superstar

Most winning teams will have their superstar or hero. Not only is this person there to carry some weight of the team, they're also there to motivate and inspire the rest of the team. In business, an obvious parallel is sales – the superstar sales person will share ideas, traits, and presentations encouraging their whole team to perform at that same high level. My own organization is constantly sharing success stories and best practices across all divisions to make sure all teams are well educated and informed.

Preparation and Hard Work

I think the average sports fan has no idea how much work professional and college athletes spend preparing in the offseason and the week before a game. I was reading a story on Peyton Manning before his last Super Bowl and it talked about the hours and hours of game tapes he would watch, not just at practice but at home, too. My friend, Graham Shuler, the starting center for Stanford mentioned looking at 3 years of game tapes in preparation for a bowl game. Preparation is just as critical in business. Are you studying your industry's "game tapes?" What preparation are you doing before a big meeting? We've been charged with having a detailed agenda before every meeting, sending it to our client ahead of time for approval, then making any changes and executing the plan. Sounds simple, but when was the last time you did the same?

Reload vs. Rebuild

Great teams don't rebuild…they reload. This common saying in sports means that teams are prepared for unforeseen events – and business as usual. My friend, DJ Kreal, often quotes Mike Tyson, *"Everyone has a plan until they get punched in the face!"* when he talks about the unexpected.

The most obvious punch in the face in sports is an injured or retiring player. In business it could be a data breech, a lost customer, or team member that jumps ship. Are you ready to reload if a business "injury" hits your team? Does it set you back to the start forcing you to rebuild? Make sure you have not only the right team members, but also great folks training and waiting in the wings when the unexpected strikes.

Stay Hungry

Last, great teams are never satisfied. As soon as the season is over, championship or not, they already have their eye on next year... planning and setting goals, executing...building that cage with a long-term vision.

Remember, after your team is in place, prepare and work hard, be ready for the unexpected... then set yourself on the road to your own championship season.

Encouragement, Time, and Competition

Fitness has always been a big part of my life – from competing in high school and collegiate sports to running half marathons, I have always been motivated to stay in shape and compete in some form or fashion. Last May, my wife and I began training at IronTribe Fitness in Brentwood – one of the fastest growing fitness franchises in the Southeast. It is group weight and cardio training with the element of team focus, competition… for time. This concept pushes every member – no matter what fitness level – to become a better athlete. We were intimidated at first not knowing what to expect, but we quickly discovered the following:

The group format allowed us to help motivate and encourage other athletes and forced us to grow as well. The competition aspect pushed us so that we worked harder to become better each and every workout. The fact that the workouts are timed made us to focus on the challenge at hand and not lolly-gag around wasting valuable time. This great athletic training concept of competition, group encouragement and time can be easily transferred to your business, career and team. Take a look at the following ways you can incorporate the IronTribe training values in your daily business life:

Competition

General Colin Powell said "The healthiest competition occurs when average people win by putting above average effort". Think about the brand new athlete at IronTribe, the new Marine at boot camp or the rookie on your team – everyone is going to hit a wall or point where they plateau out. Competition within your team will take your people and business to the next level. Integrating competition into the workplace will keep everyone's focus on the overall goal and bring the performance of the team higher than ever before. We had monthly and weekly goals for all of our staff, not just sale representatives – goals that were achievable and immediately recognized. Some people will say competition will weed out the weaker links – I disagree – it will bring out the best in everyone's overall performance.

Team Encouragement

There's the old story about the man that breaks rocks every day... all day. Someone asked him how do you do this without getting bored or tired of your job? He responds that he is not breaking rocks but making stones that will eventually build tall beautiful buildings – I am part of a team that builds something amazing. No matter what position you are in your organization we all need encouragement. Your team's success depends on the level of engagement and encouragement they receive throughout the year – make sure this is woven in the fabric of your organization.

Time

You will hear some people say the most valuable asset they have is their time. Consultants and public speakers will charge crazy hourly rates and appearance fees just to share their time. What is time worth at your organization? What is your time worth? What does wasted time mean for your customers and business? A few years ago we began putting strict timeframes on our request for proposals from vendors for our clients. We give them anywhere between 14-21 days to have the proposal back to our team for evaluation. It was amazing to see the speed at which the proposals came in, especially after we did not accept them after the deadline. Like finishing your workout in the allotted 20 minute time frame, time can be your worst enemy or a great tool – use it to your advantage.

So like the athlete at IronTribe that is getting stronger, faster and more efficient, incorporate these valuable training ideas with your business, and you too can take your team to the next level.

The Flu and Long Term Business Planning

It happened.

I never get sick. I mean, I DON'T get sick. I own a business, I *CAN'T* get sick.

I'd taken my family to the local "Doc in The Box" and we all got flu shots, but it still happened. I got the flu. For almost 4 full days, I didn't want to leave the house, or think about anything but getting better. What was going to happen next? I could only focus on my immediate future – chicken soup and Nyquil.

Luckily, I was able to work from home, my bed, even my kitchen. I could return emails, text clients or friends, and listen to voicemails. I didn't care about the mail at the office, whether or not my employees were coming in late or early...or even there. I had the flu and I was working minute-by-minute.

Day 5 and I was starting to feel better. I began thinking about the weekend and even the following week. I started returning phone calls, making appointments and closing deals. I was BACK IN THE GAME! I started thinking long-term...one month, two months ahead. And then it hit me.

As business professionals, we have to be strategic, long-term thinkers. We have to think about the big picture. Unfortunately, there are going to be times when the uncontrollable happens...like the flu.

We are often so trapped working IN our business that we forget about working ON our business.

So, what's the equivalent of a flu shot for business professionals? How can we prevent getting caught up in the routine craziness of daily work and stay focused on long-term goals?

Here are a few keys to being prepared:

Be the Best in Knowledge and Responsiveness

No matter what your business — manufacturing, service, retail, health-care, or technology — we all provide *knowledge* and *responsiveness* to our clients. Whether you have a warehouse full of inventory or you're a service provider, our clients *demand* this. We must provide customer service at our best. So, make sure you are the most knowledgeable in your field and make sure you have ways to respond to inquiries instantly. My team returns phone calls within 15 minutes and emails immediately. If we don't have an answer and are working on a problem, we give them status updates. We are in the insurance industry so our clients expect their problems solved immediately. Remember, if you don't respond to an inquiry within a few minutes, you're already weeks late…because your clients have Googled the solution and moved on.

Explore Your Expenses and Profit

Long-term goals are not achieved without an eagle eye on expenses and year-over-year profit. Too many business owners and entrepreneurs tend to bleed out expenses, grow revenue or keep revenue flat and cut expenses. It's a fine line, but with attention to both, you can find hidden profit on both sides. Start with the small expenses. Where are you spending money day-to-day that adds up? Take a hard look at your pricing and where it fits within your region, industry and competitors.

Engage in the Community

Most philanthropic and charitable events now have sponsorship opportunities or corporate team categories and challenges.

Remember, it's easy to give back to the community while you run a successful business – and it can help your business in the long term. A good friend of mine always says, "It's amazing what you can accomplish when you get a group of people together that truly care." Does this define you? Does this define your employees? Does this define your business? It should. Make it part your corporate culture.

Learn How to Grow

What we all want – what keeps us up at night – business growth. Is it a new location? Is it new employees? Is it a new product or a new strategic partner? Our long-term goals must include growth plans. When you first started your company, what was your goal and where are you now? I've found with my company that growth is a funny thing. We have grown year-by-year for six years, but in very different ways. Make sure you're always contemplating areas of growth that may be outside your area of expertise.

If there's one thing I remember from business school, it's that long-term goals have to be realistic, documented, and reviewed. Learn from the suggestions I've shared above and there's an excellent chance you'll be prepared for the unexpected...the business person's version of the flu.

How Do YOU Compete?

The insurance business is one of the most competitive industries alive.

Part of the reason is that it's relationship based. We're not selling a product, we are selling services and promises and everyone knows someone who *"knows someone"* who is in the insurance or consulting business. I can't tell you how many times I've found out that someone has spewed venom at me, my company or product in an attempt to get a leg up on a client or prospect. I swear to you that I once overheard someone saying, "There is blood in the water...it's time to strike!"

Think about it. Is this how you compete in your industry? Is this what you would want your competitors to say about you? Competition, like objects in the rear view mirror, is truly closer than it appears. I've found that taking the high road and competing against what I often call "faceless competition" is, in the long run, the best road to success.

Here are a few ideas that will keep you on top and allow you to sleep well knowing you fought a fair fight (Presidential candidates pay close attention).

Don't Bash Your Competition

Have you ever been in a social situation and someone starts bashing or talking about someone you all know? The first thing that comes to mind is...what are *they* going to say about *ME* when *I'M* not around? It's the same in business. I had a client (and close friend) tell me that several vendors had set up appointments with them. Instead of presenting their products and services, they talked about how their current vendor (ME!) was not doing the job. What chance of getting the business do they have? Zero!

Share Your Strengths

I've always believed in leading with strengths. When the topic of competition arises my response is: "They are a great company and are well respected, however, let me show you why we are different (or better)." What is wrong with that? Lead with your pricing, customer service, cost savings, experience, knowledge, product features and people...it will pay off, I promise. As a close friend often reminds me...don't wrestle with a pig...you will both get muddy and the pig will love it.

Intel is Key

The more information you amass on your competition, the stronger you'll be. There are a few great ways to do this:

- **Talk to your customers.** When you sign a new client, ask them why they left or what went wrong. Get as much information as you can.

- **Talk to your vendors and suppliers.** Not all folks will be willing to talk, but if you have a good relationship, you'll find out what's going on and what trends are out there that you might be missing.

- **Talk product information.** Make sure you're comparing apples to apples and you have the latest technical specs on all "they" are offering.

Keep Your Competiton Close

Remember the old quote attributed to Sun Tzu and used by Michael Corleone in the Godfather Part II: "Keep your friends close, and your enemies closer." Some will argue the meaning of this, but in business competition, it means the closer you are to your competitor, the more you find out about who, what, why, and where they are. Our world is small and getting smaller everyday – everyone knows everyone. Not only will keeping your competition close keep you in the game, you might even benefit from them. Some of my close friends in my industry have shared prospects and leads (and I've done the same with them) for opportunities that might not fit their niche. You never know when you might benefit from a competitor who trusts and respects you.

So, find out as much as you can about what your competitors are doing, lead with your strengths and always take the high road. I promise those objects in the rear view will not only be smaller – they'll disappear.

Management Principles

If you ask any of my sales reps or employees that have worked with me – or for me – in the past 22 years they'll probably tell you that I've mellowed out.

Ask me, though, and I'll tell you it's not so much that I've mellowed out. It's that I've learned how to manage and work with people in a much different way. I used to be militant, hard-driving and tense...because that's what I thought management was all about (think Alec Baldwin in *Glengarry Glen Ross*). Over the years I've learned that style of management can intimidate and push folks away, which ultimately hinders employee and company performance.

Instead, I've learned that it's much better to motivate or inspire. In fact, here are four tips that I've learned over the years to help do just that:

Create an Atmosphere Where Your Team Can Succeed

We used to have a saying in my office for sales reps who were stuck in the office with administrative duties instead of getting out on calls with clients...we'd say they were stuck in the "Velcro Chair." These folks were tied up with expense reports, conference calls, or other non-revenue generating distractions. As a manager, it's your job to make sure your employees have the opportunity to have the experience in front of the prospect or customer. Don't tie them down all day with items that could be handled in an alternate, more efficient manner. Instead, give them the tools and training necessary to be successful in front of the customer...it'll pay big dividends for your business, and for your employee.

Don't Overreact – Just Don't React At All

Face it now. There are going to be times in your career where you'll be ready to split apart because of an employee or situation. During one of my first college jobs I had a hot-headed manager. He'd jump the gun and overreact to situations without understanding the full story. Case in point – he almost fired the office manager because he thought she'd forgotten to FedEx an important document to a client. As it turned out, the package had been delivered, not only on time, but early – then misplaced at our client's office! In most situations, if you step back and take a deep breath, issues will work themselves out. In turn, you'll save yourself and your team a great deal of stress.

Try Transparency

Obviously there are going to be things you can't – or don't – want to share with your team. However, I've found that the more open and transparent you are, the more trusting and motivated your team will be. There's nothing worse than employees lurking around trying to figure out what's going on or whispering at the water cooler. So, make an effort to include your team in important decisions. Communicate clearly during difficult times or stressful situations like a lost client or a merger. The more your team knows and feels included, the less you'll have to worry about poor performance, wasted time, or turnover.

It's Not Three Strikes, It's Two

I'm a big believer in benefit of the doubt and giving people a second chance ... and then ... that's where it ends. The one thing I've learned the hard way is that even though we all make mistakes, once a pattern appears it's time to get concerned. This could be something as simple as being late for work, or something larger like poor performance or disrespectful behavior. If you've given your team member a chance to correct their mistakes or behavior and there's still no improvement, then it's time for a change. Trust your gut. This is business, not baseball.

Try these suggestions on for size and see if they impact your office environment. Most likely, your team will thank you for being a friend, but more importantly, a great manager and motivator.

Never Leave the Locker Room of the Super Bowl

Here's a true story.

In 1996 my friends and I managed to work our way into the Dallas Cowboys locker room after their victory over the Pittsburgh Steelers in Super Bowl XXX.

There we were. High-fiving Deion Sanders, watching Lesley Visser interview Troy Aikman, and at one point, holding the Vince Lombardi trophy. After about 45 minutes we decided to leave, thinking there might be another, better place to be. A party somewhere, maybe? But, after some time, we wound up standing behind Sun Devil Stadium thinking: "What did we just do? Did we actually just walk out of the Super Bowl locker room? AGH!"

In today's fast-paced business world we tend to always look for the next best thing. We never truly enjoy the present moment. With that in mind, here are three ways to help you, your company, and your employees stop and smell the roses.

Celebrate Wins

Whether it's a new customer, a new product, or even a business anniversary, make sure you and your employees take time to celebrate achievements regularly. This strategy will not only improve employee good will but also improve productivity.

I had the chance to tour the Zappos headquarters in Las Vegas a few years ago and they have some fantastic ways they celebrate. Zappos lauds new sales by allowing their employees to thank the customer creatively. It could be a thank you note, flowers, cookies or maybe a coupon for a future purchase – and it's the Zappos associates who decide what to send. Think about that concept – employees that buy in to the corporate goals are sure to perform at a higher level.

Recognize and Reward

My father worked in the recognition industry for almost his whole career and still consults with companies on their programs. He'll tell you that recognition is one of the easiest things you can do and it can be as important in the long run as pay and benefits, especially with tenured employees. Employee recognition will give you the best possible ROI with the least amount of time as well. Keep these rules in mind:

Individualized – employees will appreciate something that is representative of their values and beliefs (a donation to a charity of their choice for instance)

Deserved – make sure the recognition is tied to a specific goal or achievement

Timely – don't wait 3 weeks to recognize an outstanding performance – do it immediately

Reflect your culture – your recognition should embody your overall corporate goals and culture

Embrace Experiences

Think about the Tim McGraw song "My Next 30 Years." McGraw sings about slowing down and changing his behaviors moving forward. I get that. I spent the first 20 years of my career looking for the next sale, new title, pay raise, or bigger office. Today, though, my focus is on experiences … and that could be with a client, a co-worker or my family.

Who will you spend your time with and what will you be doing? My clients would much rather attend a charity or sporting event with my team than receive a tin of popcorn over the holidays. Time spent with your important relationships will pay off big. You can provide a lasting memory and be a better business owner, co-worker and family member.

My friends and I have a saying if we're having a great time and someone suggests leaving: "You never leave the locker room of the Super Bowl!" Consider the suggestions above, and you, too, can easily become a better business professional when you learn to savor the moment.

Acknowledgements

I want to thank my **ROCK STAR** editor, Amanda Kramer...she edited every single article from her phone, car, office and laptop late night for no pay

To my AP English teachers, Ruth Dunning and the late Lynn Taylor, who taught me the importance of "but, also," the "chief distracter," and the love and importance of writing

Thanks to Lance Williams, editor at *The Tennessean,* for believing in me and adding local content to the business section

To The *Make-A-Wish Foundation of Middle Tennessee* for allowing me to serve my community

Casey and Tammy Hanback who are best friends first and then family

Kimberly & Tony Young and Rob & Teri Oeding for treating me like family before I was family

Dierks and Cassidy Bentley who share our excitement of first class upgrades (compliments of Vegas) and the importance and love of family and friends

Tim and Arnita Ozgener for their unconditional friendship and love of family

Chris and Whitney Morris who have showed me the importance of making every single moment in life count

Joey and Carmen Lewis who exude friendship and love, two of the best friends, parents and people you will ever meet

Keith and Collette Rice who have showed me the importance of love and friendship

John and Lisa Henderson for their friendship and love and letting me sing at their wedding (after grandma left)

Todd Dyson for always picking up where we left off...always

Barb Shaffer and Jen Spice for taking a leap of faith with me and *THG*

Stephanie and Bill Ditenhafer for always making family and friends a priority

DJ Kreal for showing me resilience first hand and the love of family

Sid and Lola Chambless who are amazing parents and friends

John Rowley...a real life Jedi Master

Michael Haddad with whom I've shared some of the greatest trips ...ever

George Uribe for encouraging me to step outside of *my* comfort zone

Sheri Horn for being a dear friend and first client of *The Hanback Group*

Todd and Jen Kornblit, our partners in crime and *Schweddy Balls* teammates

Jon Neal who shares my love of U2 and friends (in that order)

Jae and John Robbins who are amazing parents and continue to show me the importance of family

Todd Penrod, the best horse partner, friend and cousin-in-law anyone could ask for

Terry and Michelle McKee our dear friends who we started our love and friendship with

Mark Blaze for showing me that friendship trumps time and distance, my *Wonderwall*, "I got one for you" Thanks bro...

Brian and Mallory Dillion for their unconditional love and support of our family

Chris and Joann Schott for their friendship, love, taking us in on a snowy night and giving us the "Joann Pour"

Chris and Pam Williams (Raef and Lovely) for their friendship, partnership, and love of family – let's have just one more splash...

John Dwyer and Lynley Hammes for making every experience *EPIC*

Andy Brasser for his laughter, humor and friendship – there is a family that was on that cruise ship that is still haunted by our antics...

Rob Shuler for believing in me as a business leader & friend and showing me the strength of being a great father

The original FOB's: Carol McAlpine, Jim Berry, Fletcher Foster, and Ed Lang...thank you for taking a chance on Make-A-Wish Middle of Tennessee and my leadership

Greg Hatcher for showing me the importance of taking care of the customer

Joel Brown whose book, *The Waitress Book*, inspired me to take this chance...thank you

Sadler Norris for taking a chance and following me to Nashville in 1998

Brian Donnelly for showing me the value of a positive attitude and friendship

Mike and Katy Smith for taking a risk on me & Britt and *The Hanback Group*

Doug and Kelli Hudson for their unconditional friendship

Beth Torres who reminds me that you can love what you do every…single…day

Kevin and Shima Carter for showing me that as life changes, your values and purpose don't have to

Jay Mathis who is the definition of coach and friend

Glenn T. Hays for giving me a chance to compete in the *NCAA*

Mike Griggs and Mike Parrish for taking a chance on me

Steve McSweeney for getting us in the locker room of the Super Bowl in 96' and keeping us all in stitches

Dean Munyon for picking up right where we left off, time and time again

Jim Foley for taking a chance on me right out of college

The late Coach Tommy Harrison for waking me up in study hall and asking me if I want to run the 4x400 relay as he thought we could win the state championship, and in turn, changing my life

Finally…we lost a dear friend unexpectedly. Tennessee Titan and champion of community service, Rob Bironas, was taken from this earth too soon. His jersey hangs in my office and it reads: "Ben, To more good times!"

I look up at it every day as a reminder of how precious life and friendship is

Rob Bironas and Ben Hanback

Made in the USA
Middletown, DE
26 April 2019